ADVERTISING LANGUAGE

'This clearly written book will be of interest to a wide range of people. The chapter on images of women in advertisements is particularly useful.'

Jean Aitchison, University of Oxford

Advertising has become a popular subject of study, approached from a wide range of disciplines, such as anthropology, sociology, linguistics, literary criticism, and media studies. *Advertising Language* explores the language of written advertising in Britain and Japan within the framework of pragmatics, and reveals how communication occurs between advertiser and audience.

Applying the central notions of Relevance Theory to specific adverts, Keiko Tanaka reveals how language is used to persuade, convince and manipulate others. Particular emphasis is placed on the use of puns and metaphors, and a unique chapter on images of women in Japanese advertising reveals penetrating cultural insights.

Now available in paperback, *Advertising Language* provides a compelling analysis of the language of advertising, and an exploration of Relevance Theory that will be of interest to scholars in many fields.

Keiko Tanaka is Senior Research Fellow at Hertford College, Oxford.

D0073770

ADVERTISING LANGUAGE

A pragmatic approach to
advertisements in Britain and Japan

Keiko Tanaka

London and New York

First published 1994
by Routledge
11 New Fetter Lane, London EC4P 4EE

Simultaneously published in the USA and Canada
by Routledge
29 West 35th Street, New York, NY 10001

Reprinted 1996, 1997, 1998

First published in paperback 1999

© 1994 Keiko Tanaka

Typeset in 10/12 pt Palatino by
Florencetype Ltd, Kewstoke, Avon
Printed and bound in Great Britain by
T.J. International Ltd, Padstow, Cornwall

British Library Cataloguing in Publication Data
A catalogue record for this book is available from the
British Library

Library of Congress Cataloguing in Publication Data
Tanaka, Keiko.
Advertising language: a pragmatic approach to
advertisements in Britain and Japan/Keiko Tanaka.
p. cm.
Includes bibliographical references and index.
1. Advertising–Great Britain. 2. Advertising–Japan.
3. Communication–Social aspects–Great Britain.
4. Communication–Social aspects–Japan.   I. Title.
HF5827.T35 1993
659.1′014–dc20′93–24963

ISBN 0–415–07647–1 (hbk)
ISBN 0–415–19835–6 (pbk)

To my dear little daughter,
Sophie Akiko Christine
(30 September to 2 October 1995),
Sarah's twin sister.

CONTENTS

PLATES

PREFACE TO THE
PAPERBACK EDITION

Advertising has become a popular subject of study, approached from a wide range of disciplines, such as anthropology, sociology, linguistics, literary criticism, and media studies. The main purpose of this book is to analyse the language of written advertising in Britain and Japan within the framework of pragmatics, and to explain how communication occurs between advertiser and audience. The nature of communication and how it is achieved are considered, and aspects of communication prominent in the language of advertising are investigated.

When I was casting around for a Ph.D. topic in London, I discovered Sperber and Wilson's Relevance Theory (1986a, 1995). Even before their seminal book had been published, the theory had attracted waves of intense and exciting debate in many fields of study. Reviewing their book for the *London Review of Books*, Alastair Fowler commented:

> The repercussions of *Relevance* are likely in the long run to be great – felt first, perhaps, in the pragmatics of conversation, the philosophy of language, and reader-response criticism, but also in many other activities: construction of memory models, pedagogy machine learning and (doubtless) advertising and propaganda.

The hardback version of my book was the first monograph to take up this challenge, exploring various aspects of the language used in advertising from the viewpoint of Relevance Theory.

My exploration of advertising is part of a more general investigation into the force of language, more specifically the way language is used to persuade, convince, and manipulate others. The examples used by Sperber and Wilson are mainly concerned with situations in which communication occurs between trusting and equal

xi

partners. Much of my work, in contrast, attempts to apply the central notions of Relevance Theory to the very different social situation that characterises advertising.

The first part of the book surveys and criticises selected approaches to the language of advertising, and puts forward Relevance Theory as the best basis for explaining the comprehension of utterances. I then go on to investigate selected topics in the language of advertising, which might seem to pose problems for Relevance Theory.

The partial suppression of the advertiser's intentions in 'covert communication' and punning appears problematic at first sight. Sperber and Wilson's analysis of communication is based on a model which involves the speaker letting it be known that he is trying to communicate something. There are forms of communication that fall outside this model. Punning appears to be a counter-example for Relevance Theory, whereby the audience is expected by the speaker not only to recover the first interpretation which comes to their mind, but also to go on and recover the second interpretation. Nevertheless, it is argued that Relevance Theory provides valuable insights and useful explanations as to how such forms of communication are achieved. The distinction between the informative intention, the intention to inform the audience of something, and the communicative intention, that is, the intention to reveal this informative intention, is crucial in accounting for covert communication. The audience's interest in cost-effectiveness, and its search for 'optimal relevance', prove to be vital in understanding how communication works when there are two or more interpretations involved, specifically in the case of pun.

Metaphors in advertising, and the extended use of words in the projection of the image of women in advertisements, are less problematic, but contribute to the analysis of the force of language in advertising. The notion of 'loose' use of language is the key to their understanding. When the proposition expressed by an utterance is identical with the thought it represents, it is described as 'literal'. However, when the proposition expressed by an utterance resembles the thought it represents only to some degree, the utterance is 'loose'. Loose use of language is rife in ordinary communication, whereas strictly literal use is rare. Unless there is a specific reason to believe that an utterance is literal, the hearer assumes that there is some degree of looseness present. Metaphor and the selected keywords describing women in advertising are just two examples of such use of language.

ACKNOWLEDGEMENTS

My special gratitude goes to Deirdre Wilson for all her support and encouragement over the years and for her useful comments and advice on earlier drafts of this book. Without her generous help, this book could not have been written. If I remain unenlightened, the fault is entirely mine.

Three other people gave me strong academic and moral support. As my supervisor, Ruth Kempson steered to its completion the Ph.D. thesis upon which this book is based, while Robyn Carston gave me friendly support and provided me with useful comments on earlier drafts. I owe a particular debt of gratitude to Samya Bencherif, with whom I spent numerous stimulating hours discussing Relevance Theory, as we jointly worked on covert communication, she in the political sphere and I in advertising. Since Samya's return to Algeria, we have lost touch, perhaps due to the tense political situation in that country. I hope that she may find this book somewhere, and that it will stimulate her to complete her thesis and take up her work in this area once again. I count it a great privilege to have worked with these scholars, but, again, the remaining faults in this book are entirely mine.

I also wish to express my gratitude to those who made it possible for me to embark on writing a Ph.D. thesis at all. Jojiro Kishida taught me English at Kobe City University of Foreign Studies and encouraged me to come to Britain to study linguistics. He shared with me his infectious excitement about linguistics, and made it mine. Patrick Hanks supervised me at the University of Essex for my M.A. He taught me the joy of studying linguistics, and, indeed, the joy of studying in general. Had I not met those people, this book would not even have been started. I stand indebted to them.

My heartfelt gratitude goes to my family, and especially to my late grandmother, Hatsue Akutagawa, who gave me financial support to start a Ph.D., and to my two mentors, my mother, Kazuko Tanaka, and my late aunt, Takako Takizawa, for their support and encouragement. The family members who particularly encouraged me to engage in graduate study and become an academic were all women to whom higher education had been denied. Their husbands and brothers went to university, but they were forced to play a domestic role because of lack of opportunities. My grandfather went to university, but two generations later, I was the first woman in the family to be able to go to university, let alone write a Ph.D. I am extremely grateful that the women in my family gave me so much encouragement to grasp an opportunity which they had themselves never been able to take up.

Last but not least, I wish to thank my husband William Tanaka (Clarence-Smith) for his manifold support, which ranged from being my sounding-board, commenting on drafts, proof-reading, doing housework and looking after Sarah since her arrival in September 1995, a most enjoyable but not always easy task, and coping with my moods. I sincerely hope that spending so much time and energy on this book has not kept him away from his own writing.

For this paperback edition, I would like to express my gratitude to colleagues and students at Oxford who have given me encouragement since my arrival in the autumn of 1993. Jean Aitchison and Susanne Romaine in the Sub-Faculty of Linguistics and Philology have given me general support, and their joint lectures on metaphor were highly stimulating. The students who attended my lectures on 'Language of the British and Japanese media' asked awkward questions and made many interesting comments. I hope that they enjoyed hearing the lectures as much as I enjoyed giving them. They have made me want to go on working on the subject. All the remaining shortcomings, however, are mine alone.

PRELIMINARY NOTES

Gender: Contrary to Sperber and Wilson's usage, I systematically consider the speaker to be male and the hearer to be female, on the grounds that advertisers are nearly always men and that their target audiences tend to be women (Dyer 1982:83). This is in no way to suggest that women should in a general sense play a passive role, but this usage may represent common situations in which male advertisers depict women in ways discussed in this book.

Japanese transcription: Vowel sequences in Japanese, such as *aa*, *ii*, and *oo*, are frequently considered to be long vowels. A true long vowel, however, can only be assigned a prominence, that is, high tone or stress, on its initial element. But it is possible for the second element of a so-called long vowel in Japanese to bear such prominence. Therefore, following Yoshida (1990), they are written as sequences of two vowels.

Abbreviations used in glosses

ACC	accusative	HON	honorific
ADV	adverb(ialiser)	NEG	negation
CAUS	causative	NOM	nominative
COMP	complementiser	PASS	passive
COP	copula	PAST	past
EMPH	emphatic	PERF	perfective
FP	final particle	PL	plural
GEN	genitive	TOP	topic

1

ADVERTISING
AND COMMUNICATION

INTRODUCTION

There has long been interest in the means employed by advertisers to communicate with their audience. This chapter assesses
how the problems raised by the language of advertising have
been approached. It is my contention that those who have
written on this subject have not dealt adequately with the question of the context within which an audience processes an
advertisement. Conversely, they have relied too much on 'system of signs' in the text. This chapter reviews a selection of
theories in semiotics and linguistics which provides insights into
the problem. At the same time, the defects of these theories are
examined from the point of view of the contribution made by
Relevance Theory (Sperber and Wilson 1986a, 1995).

SOME SEMIOTIC APPROACHES

Semiotic approaches are based on the assumption that communication is achieved by encoding and decoding a message,
and Barthes is one of the most distinguished scholars to have
tackled the language of advertising from such a perspective. His
'Rhetoric of the image' (1984b) is claimed by Dyer (1982: 224) to
be a major essay on semiotics and its application to the analysis
of an advertising message. In this stimulating but ultimately
unsatisfactory text Barthes studies the interrelationships between the image and the advertising message, using as an
example an advertisement for a kind of pasta called Panzani.

Barthes argues that there are three kinds of message: the
linguistic message, the coded iconic message, and the non-

1

coded iconic message. The linguistic message consists of the caption and the labels. Barthes points out that there exist two levels of interpretation of the linguistic message, namely, denotational and connotational. The name of the advertised product denotes the pasta, and connotes 'Italianicity'. Putting aside the linguistic message, Barthes argues that we are left with the pure image. This is divided into two categories, which are the iconic equivalents of connotation and denotation. The former is also categorised as a coded, symbolic, and cultural message, while the latter is said to be the non-coded, perceptual and literal message. Barthes' insight that one can derive different pieces of information from a single advertisement is valuable, but the way in which he sets out to analyse it is problematic.

The denotation-connotation distinction is not clear-cut, at either the linguistic or the iconic level, because perceptual information is not independent of cultural knowledge. As Fodor (1983) points out, a distinction between 'central' thought processes and 'perceptual' processes is assumed in current cognitive psychology. Perceptual systems are said to transform information from sensory representations into conceptual representations. The information received by such input systems, however, 'underdetermines' (Fodor 1983: 68) the information derived from them by the central thought processes. In other words, the central thought processes integrate information derived from the senses with information stored in memory to determine what is actually perceived. Thus, even the processing of information derived from the senses is affected by cultural knowledge.

The thesis that different messages are disentangled solely by reading systems of signs runs up against the problem that there exist a potentially infinite number of different messages carried by a finite number of signs. Barthes is clearly aware of this difficulty. He attempts to resolve it by arguing that the linguistic message has a function *vis-à-vis* the iconic message, a function which he calls 'anchorage', that is the determination of the selection of the intended message:

> . . . all images are polysemous . . . [which] poses a question of meaning and this question always comes through as a dysfunction even if this dysfunction is recuperated by society as a tragic . . . or a poetic game . . . [The

caption] helps me to choose *the correct level of perception*, permits me to focus not simply my gaze but also my understanding.

(Barthes 1984b: 38–9, author's italics)

The problem with this proposed solution is that linguistic messages are also polysemous. However much we would like them to be clear and straightforward, linguistic codes are not devoid of ambiguity. Reference assignment, disambiguation and enrichment are part of the normal process of utterance interpretation (Sperber and Wilson 1986a: 185).

Moreover, Barthes' account fails to explain the popularity in advertising of such linguistic devices as the pun, where the linguistic message is intentionally polysemous. Indeed, it is doubtful whether advertisers in Britain and Japan regard the polysemous nature of linguistic and non-linguistic messages as a 'tragedy'. On the contrary, as is argued in Chapter 4, the advantage of puns, which are frequently exploited in advertising, lies in their potential multiplicity of meanings. They are eye-catching and can thus sustain an audience's attention for a longer period of time.

The emphasis which Barthes (1984b: 34-5) places on the discontinuity between different signs causes further problems. He concludes that there are four discontinuous connotational signs in the advertisement in question: (a) a suggestion of a return from the market implies the freshness of the products and domestic preparation; (b) the colours used in the poster mean 'Italianicity'; (c) the serried collection of different objects suggests the idea of a total culinary service; (d) the composition of the objects implies the image of a still-life painting. But why are the freshness of the products and the domestic preparation categorised as one message, while the idea of a culinary service is placed in a separate category? The division seems arbitrary. The number of signs attributed by Barthes to the illustration appears equally arbitrary, for he does not provide any criteria for determining how many signs there might be. It would surely be possible for an audience to derive further messages from the advertisement in question, for example ideas of harvest and abundance.

Moreover, Barthes' analysis would completely fail to provide an adequate account for other advertisements. How would he 'read' the discontinuous connotational messages of the advertisements in a controversial Benetton series, which show, *inter alia*, a dying Aids patient, a victim of the Mafia, an electric chair, and a blazing car? These illustrations have no obvious connection with Benetton clothes. Many advertisements for Silk Cut cigarettes in Britain do not even show the brand name, and the only linguistic message is the government health warning at the bottom. The appreciation of such advertisements involves more than decoding their linguistic and iconic messages.

As for Barthes' contention that it is possible to talk of explicit, discontinuous messages, this stems from a more general claim that language is the prime example of a semiological system (Culler 1983a: 73), whereas Sperber and Wilson (1986a: 55) maintain that the kind of explicit communication that can be achieved by the use of language is not a typical but a limiting case. While it is reasonable to argue that linguistic communication is capable of achieving a degree of precision and complexity unattainable by non-linguistic communication, the communicator does not always intend to communicate a finite number of explicit and precise messages. Instead, he provides evidence for a range of conclusions, which become more accessible to the audience to varying degrees. The thoughts which are communicated by advertisements seem to be as richly structured as the sentences used to communicate them, and much more so than the systems of signs proposed by semioticians.

Another semiotician who provides a stimulating but problematic approach to the language of advertising is Judith Williamson (1983). She analyses a Goodyear tyre advertisement, which shows a jetty on which a car is apparently being tested for its braking performance. She argues that, on the 'manifest' level, the jetty signifies the test of braking power and connotes 'risk', but on the 'latent' level, it signifies 'tyre' because of their similarity in appearance, and connotes 'safety' (Williamson 1983: 19). She goes on to say:

> this transference of significance does not exist as completed in the ad, but requires us to *make* the connection: it is nowhere stated that the tyre is as strong as the jetty, therefore this meaning does not exist until we complete the transference ourselves.
>
> (Williamson 1983: 19, author's italics)

Williamson has nearly stumbled on the fact that advertising

4

messages are not fully encoded and that interpreting advertisements takes more than just decoding. They need the audience to make appropriate connections. Williamson's way of resolving the dilemma is unsatisfactory, although she begins to seize the importance of context. She presents an additional system of meaning, arguing that the 'transference' is 'based on the fact that the first object (jetty) *has* a significance to be transferred' (Williamson 1983: 19, author's italics):

> the advertisement does not create meaning initially but invites us to make a transaction where it is passed from one thing to another. A system of meaning must already exist in which jetties are seen as strong, and this system is exterior to the ad – which simply *refers* to it, using one of its components as a carrier of value (in the case of [the example above], strength, durability) – i.e. as a currency.
>
> (Williamson 1983: 19, author's italics)

She calls this mechanism the 'referent system' (1983: 19) and goes on to define 'currency' as follows:

> Currency is something which represents a value and in its inter-changeability with other things, gives them their 'value' too.
>
> (Williamson 1983: 20)

Pateman (1983) correctly rejects Williamson's argument as unsound. For a currency which allows the jetty-strength connection to exist, there have to be an infinite number of such systems. Williamson herself notes that the jetty represents risk as well as strength. She may well be right in saying that the jetty in the advertisement represents both risk and strength. However, she does not explain how an audience will know which system is valid, the jetty as risk, the jetty as strength or indeed yet another system.

This is especially problematic when, according to Williamson, the jetty as risk system is used on the 'manifest' level and the jetty as strength system on the 'latent' level. How is an audience to know which system is to be used and when? She points out herself that there is nothing in the advertisement written to the effect that the jetty stands for anything. It is not clear how an audience is supposed to select these two valid systems out of all the possible systems and use them at the right level. Nor are the criteria clear which an audience has to employ in choosing the correct currency. Williamson fails to come to grips with these essential questions.

Certainly, Williamson is aware that, for communication to succeed, the audience must be involved in carrying out a task of processing, and that there is a gap between the message which is obtained by decoding and the message which the audience actually recovers. She argues that the gap is filled by the audience's knowledge, and she goes on to assert that 'systems of knowledge' (Williamson 1983: 99) are themselves governed by rules:

> To fill in gaps we must know what to fill in, to decipher and solve problems we must know the rules of the game. Advertisements clearly produce knowledge . . . but this knowledge is always produced from something already known, that acts as a guarantee, in its anteriority, for the *'truth'* in the ad itself.
>
> (Williamson 1983: 99, author's italics)

According to Williamson (1983: 100), 'the assumption of pre-existing bodies of knowledge' allows the reference system to work. However, the question is what criteria does the audience use in order to choose relevant information from the whole range of knowledge it has? Williamson adds that her concern is to discover which precise references to pre-existing bodies of knowledge are applied in advertising. It is certainly worth investigating what ideologies advertisers employ, and Williamson's analysis is pertinent from this perspective. However, she is unable to answer her own crucial question as to how pre-existing bodies of knowledge play a role in determining the way in which advertisements are understood.

SOME LINGUISTIC APPROACHES

Vestergaard and Schrøder's *The Language of Advertising* (1985) is a recent work which illuminates one aspect of the question by arguing that advertisers take a certain behaviour or attitude as the norm, without explicitly saying so. They illustrate this with the following example, which is a caption for a foot deodorant advertisement:

(1) There was a time when no one used an underarm deodorant either.

(Vestergaard and Schrøder 1985: 141)

This advertisement tries to establish that the use of foot deodorants should be as necessary and normal as the use of underarm deodorants by drawing a parallel between them. According to Vestergaard and Schrøder, the caption in (1) not only illustrates the phenomenon of 'implied behavioural nomalcy' (Vestergaard and Schrøder 1985: 142), but also provides a clear example of 'problem reduction'. Rather than solving the problem of smelly feet by dealing with the source of the smell, the caption offers a product which neutralises the symptoms and makes the audience dependent on the product. Vestergaard and Schrøder go on to argue that advertisers need both mechanisms in their endeavour to persuade their audiences that needs can be fulfilled and problems solved through consumption.

The problem is that Vestergaard and Schrøder call these mechanisms 'semantic processes' (Vestergaard and Schrøder 1985: 145) whereas they are really pragmatic ones. Here it is necessary to consider the distinction between semantics and pragmatics. Within the framework of Relevance Theory (Blakemore 1987, 1992, and Carston, forthcoming), semantics is defined as having to do with elements of meaning which can be directly obtained from the linguistic content alone, that is, the grammar and the lexicon. Semantic meaning is obtainable by decoding linguistic expressions, and it remains valid independently of context. Pragmatics, in contrast, has to do with elements which depend on extra-linguistic contextual information and the hearer's inferential abilities.

Pateman, whose critique of Williamson was noted above, favours a pragmatic approach over one based on semiotics. He argues that semioticians take for granted 'important conditions of possibility of the routine accomplishment' (1983: 187). By 'the routine accomplishment', he means not only the audience's linguistic knowledge, but also assumptions about the communicator's intention, the principles of conversation, activity type, and the point or purpose of particular forms of communication. He notes that advertisements are 'rarely identified *in isolation* and *retrospectively* but rather they are identified *in a context* where they have been *anticipated*' (Pateman 1983: 188, his italics). He argues that unless an advertisement is identified as an advertisement it would be 'strictly impossible for us to understand . . . it' (1983: 189).

However, a text can be identified as an advertisement without any prior knowledge that it is one, even though advertisements tend to appear where they are anticipated and knowledge that something is an advertisement may help an audience to understand it. It is possible to read a text thinking at first that it is an article, and then to find out as one reads it that it is in fact an advertisement. Indeed, certain advertisements in newspapers and magazines are deliberately intended to mimic the style and graphics of the articles around them. It is plausible to say that when the prior information that something is an advertisement exists, it can act as part of the context against which the advertisement is comprehended. However, the prior information that something is an advertisment is not a prerequisite for understanding it as such.

Pateman further argues that knowledge about what kind of thing fills a slot can be used to analyse the particular object in that slot. He borrows the notion of 'activity type' from Levinson (1979), defined as follows:

> . . . I take the notion of an activity type to refer to a fuzzy category whose focal members are goal-defined, socially constituted, bounded events with *constraints* on participants, setting and so on, but above all on the kinds of allowable contribution. Paradigm examples would be teaching, a job interview, a jural interrogation, a football game, a task in a workshop, a dinner party, and so on.
> (Levinson 1979: 368, author's italics)

Pateman adds advertising to this list. He argues that participants in different activity types are prepared with minimal knowledge about the activity in which they are engaged, which includes the purpose of the activity. He continues that in the case of advertising the purpose is to sell products, and that without this knowledge an advertisement is not understandable.

There are considerable problems with this formulation. For example, the goals of a dinner party are by no means clear. Being sociable and not offending anyone are little more than a vague and arbitrary set of 'dos and don'ts'. Nor does Levinson prove his point by referring to a court case in which an alleged rape victim has just admitted prior sexual involvement with two men, at which point the defence lawyer says to her: 'And you are seventeen and a half?' The implication is that a young girl who has already slept with two men is not a woman of a good repute (1979: 380–1). But this is not a convincing argument to support the notion of activity type, for such a statement does not have to come from a lawyer in a criminal court in order to suggest this meaning. This example may reveal something about the tactics of lawyers, but it does not explain how people understand utterances.

Pateman's category of goal-defined activity also suffers from a lack of recognition that advertising is in reality socially 'goal-divided'. The goal of an advertisement is not shared by the audience, inasmuch as the different parties are striving for different social goals. The ultimate purpose of an advertiser is to change the thinking of uninterested persons in his audience and make them buy his product. If they would have bought it anyway, the advertisement is so much wasted effort. Thus if advertisers are to depend entirely upon their audience's recognition of their goal, their chances of success will be slim.

Sperber and Wilson (1987b: 742) argue that it is a step forward to recognise the importance of goals, purposes, plans, and so on, but that little progress has been made in developing adequate goal-based accounts of communication. If the speaker's goals affect the comprehension process, then some account must be provided of how the hearer can recognise these goals, and exactly how this recognition can affect the processes of disambiguation, reference assignment and understanding of metaphors, which are at the heart of comprehension.

Geis' contribution to the subject (1982) is a compelling attempt to grapple with the problem. One can distinguish three strands in his work. He builds on the notion, deriving ultimately from Grice (1957), that inference rather than decoding is the key to comprehension. Secondly he incorporates the notion of co-operation in a conversation put forward by Grice (1975), making use of six 'maxims' adapted from Grice (1975) and from Boer and Lycan (1975):

The Maxim of Strength: Say no less than is necessary.
The Maxim of Parsimony: Say no more than is necessary.

The Maxim of Truth: Do not say what you believe to be false.
The Maxim of Evidence: Do not say that for which you lack
adequate evidence.
The Maxim of Relevance: Be relevant.
The Maxim of Clarity: Avoid obscurity of expression.

(Geis 1982: 31)

Thirdly, Geis takes a formal pragmatist's viewpoint in that he
believes that problems in interpretation can be solved by the
formulation of sets of rules and scales, such as those governing
the relative 'strength' or 'weakness' of utterances.

Geis analyses American television advertisements and begins
by arguing that advertisers should be held responsible for
any non-idiosyncratic inferences which are drawn by their
audiences. More specifically, he maintains that advertisers
should be accountable for what their advertisements implicate,
as well as what their advertisements assert, for ordinary people
cannot be expected to 'distinguish between valid and invalid
inferences' (1982: 33).

His suggestion that advertisers should be held responsible for
conversational implicatures, that is the intended implications of
what they say, is in itself a reasonable proposition, but his
analysis does not provide a successful basis for implementing
such measures. He claims that conversational implicatures are
calculated as follows:

A sentence *S conversationally* implies a proposition *P* in a
given conversation if and only if *P* can be 'calculated' given

a   the literal meaning of *S*,
b   general principles governing conversation,
c   the context of the conversation,
d   background knowledge shared by speaker and hearer.

(Geis 1982: 30)

However, he does not show how the context is determined, nor
does he demonstrate how 'background knowledge shared by
speaker and hearer' is established. Without those notions being
clearly understood, it would be impossible to hold an advertiser
responsible for the conversational implicatures of what he says.
An advertiser can always deny an accusation by saying that he
was not aware that his viewers shared a particular piece of
knowledge.

Geis is aware of the difficulties which arise from the inter-relation among his maxims. He gives as an example an advertisement for Aftate, a deodorant for feet:

(2) Aftate for Athlete's foot, with a medication that kills athlete's foot fungus on contact.

(Geis 1982: 55)

Geis argues that it is implied that Aftate kills athlete's foot fungus on contact, and that the Maxim of Relevance is responsible for this intended implication. However, taking into consideration the Maxim of Strength and the fact that advertisers make the strongest claim they can in their advertisements, the fact that it is never actually claimed that Aftate kills the fungus on contact implies that Aftate may not in fact kill it on contact.

Geis tries to get round this problem by setting up a hierarchy among his maxims:

In general, the Maxims of Strength and Relevance can give rise to quite different implicatures . . . in general consumers are much more likely to go with the Maxim of Relevance than with the Maxim of Strength, for in such cases the latter requires much more sophisticated reasoning than does the former.

(Geis 1982: 55-6)

In effect, Geis is suggesting that the Maxim of Relevance is superior to that of Strength in the hierarchy of maxims. Wilson and Sperber (1981b) have gone further and shown that different maxims are not independently necessary and that they should be reduced to a single principle, that of Relevance.

From the perspective of formal pragmatics, Geis also tries to measure the relative 'strength' of claims made by advertisers, as in the following example:

(3) . . . a remarkable nasal spray that lasts and lasts up to 12 continuous hours.

(Geis 1982: 3)

This caption claims that the nasal spray remains effective for twelve hours at most, which is weaker than just saying that it lasts for twelve hours. Based on the assumption that advertisers will make the strongest claims that they can possibly defend,

11

Geis (1982: 4) concludes that the advertiser of the nasal spray cannot justify the stronger claim. Geis' proposed solution to this problem is to offer scales to measure the strength of claims, for example, strength of probability and modal verbs. Thus, supposing that John Jones is known by 100 women, it can be claimed that he is liked by many women if and only if he is liked by between 50 per cent and 75 per cent of the women.

This definition is too specific, and at the same time unrealistic, for it lacks an adequate account of the nature and role of context. Situations can easily be imagined in which Geis' formula would not work. The example of John Jones still applies if there are ninety-nine women involved, but it would not apply if the number of women were to be cut to three. Even if nearly 70 per cent of the three women liked John Jones, it could not be claimed that many women liked John Jones. A scale which is valid in one imaginary context but not in another is of little utility.

Geis correctly argues that problems of utterance interpretation should be dealt with in the framework of pragmatics, but in the ultimate analysis his approach suffers from the defects of Gricean and formal pragmatics. Geis attempts to explain utterance comprehension by adding rules of pragmatic interpretation, to which it is always possible to find counter-examples. At the same time, he does not account for the role of context in utterance comprehension.

CONCLUSION

In this chapter, selected approaches to the language used in advertising have been assessed. It has been shown that understanding advertisements is not merely a matter of decoding, and that the interpretation of advertisements is best approached from a pragmatic point of view. However, it has also been suggested that pragmatists who have analysed advertisements do not present a convincing and thorough account of the nature and role of context. Instead they attempt to make use of notions of goal-bounded activities or sets of rules, which are demonstrably insufficient to explain how audiences understand advertisements. In short, existing approaches to the language of advertising share the defects of the theories of communication on which they are based.

In contrast, Sperber and Wilson offer a principled account in *Relevance* (1986a, 1995) of how an utterance is interpreted by the hearer in context, integrating that which is worth preserving from the other approaches surveyed in this chapter. Relevance Theory provides the most satisfactory answer to the basic question of how communication is achieved in advertising, and the following chapter is thus devoted to a general exposition of Relevance Theory.

2

COMMUNICATION

INTRODUCTION

An approach to the problems of utterance interpretation based on Relevance Theory is presented in this chapter, and it will serve as the theoretical foundation for the analysis of the various aspects of advertising discussed in subsequent chapters. My recourse to this theory of communication, developed by Dan Sperber and Deirdre Wilson, springs from dissatisfaction with existing analyses of the language of advertising, as outlined in the previous chapter. In particular, Relevance Theory provides a fully formulated theory of context, which is lacking in earlier analyses.

At the most general level, Sperber and Wilson (1986a: 2) argue that it is thoughts which are communicated. By thoughts, they mean mental representations, which hearers are capable of entertaining and believing. In other words, thoughts take the form of sets of assumptions. The ultimate goal of the communicator is to alter his hearer's thoughts, and that is why he engages in communication at all.

COMMUNICATION AND INFERENCE

Recent works in psycholinguistics, pragmatics, and the philosophy of language show that there is a gap between the semantic representations of a sentence which the speaker uses and the thought which the speaker intends to communicate. This is illustrated by the following examples:

(1) It is strange.

(2)   The food is too hot.

(3)   Come back early in the morning.

'It' in (1) has to be assigned to an appropriate referent from an infinite number of possible referents. The word 'hot' can mean either 'having a high temperature' or 'spicy', and the hearer of (2) has to decide which meaning the word has in the context. Moreover, she has to know for what or for whom the food is too hot. 'Early' in (3) is vague and the understanding of the sentence is not completed until the hearer decides what time the speaker means by this. Furthermore, a sentence such as (2) can be used with a certain tone of voice by the speaker, either to complain to the hearer that the food is too hot, or to ask the hearer whether it is too hot. In such examples the linguistic form of the sentence does not provide sufficient help for the hearer to be able to identify the speaker's attitude.

Given that a sentence can be used with various non-linguistic properties, it follows that the same *sentence* can be used in different *utterances*, which result in different interpretations. The hearers in examples (1) to (3) are left with the gap between the linguistic representations of the sentence and the interpretations which the different utterances are used to convey. There are always various possibilities in any situation, and the hearer has to select one interpretation among others. The semantic representation of the sentence does not provide sufficient information for the hearer to achieve a complete interpretation of an utterance in context. Thus utterance interpretation cannot be fully accounted for in terms of semantic rules, that is as part of grammar.

It is common for the sentence meaning to 'underdetermine' the utterance meaning, although the speakers of (1) to (3) do not necessarily intend these utterances to be ambiguous. Nor are the respective hearers usually aware of any ambiguity, as it is almost invariably resolvable in context. Indeed, unless the ambiguity is resolved, the utterance will not succeed as a vehicle for communication. The distinction between this kind of resolvable ambiguity and unresolvable ambiguity, or equivocation, is important for the analysis in Chapter 4.

The gap between the linguistically encoded meaning of a sentence and what is actually communicated by uttering the sentence on a given occasion is filled by *inference*, and not by more coding. It was Grice (1957) who first drew attention to the importance of inference in communication. Various pragmatists have since developed inferential models of communication, partly along lines suggested by Grice in his later work (1975).

Inferential processes are directed towards interpreting the communicator's intention, which is a radically different process from that of decoding. In decoding a sentence, phonetic representations of sentences are encoded, and semantic representations of sentences are decoded. The input to the decoding process is a signal and the output is a message, which is paired to the signal by the underlying code.

A deductive inference is a formal operation which takes propositions as premises and yields propositions as conclusions. Given a set of deductive rules, and given a set of premises, the deductive conclusions do not vary. A set of conclusions are automatically generated. They need not therefore be stored separately. Thus, a deductive system would provide a significant economy of storage.

It is widely accepted among pragmatists that the process of inferential comprehension is usually *non-demonstrative*, as opposed to demonstrative. That is to say that the interpretation recovered from an utterance cannot be deduced directly from the content of the utterance or the discourse in which the utterance appears, and the interpretation is only likely to be correct, rather than guaranteed to be correct. Indeed, it may turn out to be wrong. The following example illustrates this point:

(4) (a) She: Would you come to dinner tonight?
    (b) He: I'm baby-sitting tonight.

In normal circumstances, the hearer of (4b) would add (5) to the context and conclude (6):

(5) If one is baby-sitting, one will be unable to come to dinner.
(6) He won't come to dinner tonight.

Thus (6) is not deducible from the content of (4) alone. Conclusion (8) is not in contradiction with (4b) if premise (7) is added to the context:

(7) If one is baby-sitting, one will bring the baby with one to dinner.

(8) He is baby-sitting tonight, and he will come to dinner with the baby tonight.

Many pragmatists (Bach and Harnish 1979; Brown and Yule 1983; Leech 1983; Levinson 1983) therefore argue that deductive processes have little or nothing to do with non-demonstrative inferential processes. These pragmatists have no clear theory of non-demonstrative reasoning, and do not offer any positive alternative to deductive inference.

Sperber and Wilson disagree. In their view, utterance interpretation involves forming a hypothesis on the basis of the input and evaluating it against other assumptions external to the discourse in question. But, whereas deductive inferences are valid in all contexts, non-demonstrative inferences are not. Depending on whether the context includes the premises (5) or (7), the different conclusions (6) and (8) respectively will be reached. However, (5) and (7) are not equally likely to be accessed. There is a criterion according to which the hearer accesses one rather than the other, as is shown below.

Grice goes on to draw attention to different intentions involved in communication, but his definition of intentionality remains ambiguous. To understand this problem, it is useful to consider the reformulation of Grice's position by Strawson (1971) in terms of 'sub-intentions'. For Strawson, there are three sub-intentions on the part of speaker: (a) the speaker makes an utterance x, intending to inform her of y and produce a response from her; (b) the speaker intends the hearer to recognise his intention to inform her of y; (c) the speaker intends the hearer's recognition of his intention to inform her of y to play a part in her response.

The problem is that it is not clear whether y in the formulation above needs to be believed by the hearer. This can be illustrated by the following example. The speaker thought that he had studied hard the night before and wanted to communicate the fact by saying:

(9) I studied hard last night.

There are situations in which the hearer might recognise that the speaker intends to inform her of this fact, but nevertheless does not believe it. For example, she may have seen him at a party the night before, and therefore she may not be convinced that he studied hard on the night in question. In other words, it is possible that the speaker's intention to inform will be recognised without being fulfilled. The speaker will still have succeeded in communication, even though he will have failed to convince his hearer. This point is dealt with in more detail in the following chapter, in relation to the function of trust in communication.

Sperber and Wilson modify the Grice-Strawson position by arguing that the intention to inform does not need to be fulfilled for communication to succeed. Thus, the intention to inform cannot correctly be described as a communicative intention. Instead, they call it an 'informative intention'. True communicative intention is the intention to have the informative intention recognised.

The goal of communication is best described as changing the *cognitive environment* of a hearer, cognitive environment being defined (Sperber and Wilson 1986a: 39) as a set of facts which are *manifest* to an individual. Manifest is in turn defined (Sperber and Wilson 1986a: 39) to mean mentally representable and acceptable as true or probably true. To be manifest is to be perceptible or inferable, and this definition of manifest entails that assumptions are manifest to varying degrees. A communicator may form a certain design on his audience, but the extent of his control over his addressee is questionable, and is certainly a matter of degree. He may not have much control over her actual thoughts, but he may have more control over the set of assumptions which are manifest to her, that is her cognitive environment. So the communicator's informative intention is better described as an intention to modify the addressee's cognitive environment, rather than as an intention directly to modify the thoughts of the addressee. However, he hopes that changing the hearer's cognitive environment will ultimately lead to the alteration of her thoughts.

OSTENSIVE-INFERENTIAL COMMUNICATION

Sperber and Wilson's analysis focuses on the form of communication which they call *ostensive-inferential* (1986a: 63), which is defined as follows:

The communicator produces a stimulus which makes it

mutually manifest to communicator and audience that the communicator intends, by means of this stimulus, to make manifest or more manifest to the audience a set of assumptions {*I*}.

(Sperber and Wilson 1986a: 63)

Ostensive-inferential communication is by definition 'overt' (Sperber and Wilson 1986a: 30) because it involves mutual manifestness. However, the distinction between informative intention and communicative intention is also of crucial significance in characterising covert communication. This lies at the heart of the discussion of covert forms of communication in Chapter 3.

'Ostention' consists of the revelation of two layers of information. The initial layer is the information which the speaker points out to the hearer. The second layer consists of the speaker indicating that he has intentionally pointed out the first piece of information to the hearer. The two types of intention are defined as follows:

Informative intention: to make manifest or more manifest to the audience a set of assumptions {*I*}.

(Sperber and Wilson 1986a: 58)

Communicative intention: to make it mutually manifest to audience and communicator that the communicator has this informative intention {*I*}.

(Sperber and Wilson 1986a: 61)

In order to succeed in communication, the communicator must attract the audience's attention, so that an act of ostension can be described as a request for attention. For example, if I point out a pit-bull terrier to my friend, in other words if I engage in an act of ostention, my behaviour raises in her the expectation that my gesture indicates that I think that there is something there worthy of her attention. My friend might already have seen the dog without paying any particular attention to it, because she was unaware that this was the infamous breed about which there had been so much talk in the newspapers. However, the fact that I pointed out the dog would suggest to my friend that I intended to draw her attention to some particular aspect of the situation which was worthy of her attention, for instance that she might be in danger of being savagely attacked.

19

The principal significance of ostensive communication is that it bears a guarantee of relevance. Human beings automatically pay attention to ostensive stimuli, because they are conditioned to turn their attention to what seems most relevant to them (Sperber and Wilson 1986a: 50). When ostensively addressed, the hearer pays attention to the speaker in a way she would not do if she happened to overhear him talking to somebody else on the phone. Even when somebody is verbally abusing you, you automatically process what is being said.

Since processing information requires effort, the request to undertake the task has to be accompanied by reward. By requesting the addressee's attention, the communicator indicates that he has reason to believe that he is providing some relevant information which will make her effort worth her while.

STANDARDS IN COMMUNICATION

For Grice, inferential communication is achieved by the use of a 'Co-operative Principle', together with maxims, a position which he expounded in his William James Lectures, delivered in 1967 (Grice 1975: 45–6). These can be set out as follows :

Co-operative Principle: Make your conversational contribution such as is required, at the stage at which it occurs, by the accepted purpose or direction of the talk exchange in which you are engaged.

Maxims of conversation
A Quantity
    1 Make your contribution as informative as is required (for the current purpose of the exchange).
    2 Do not make your contribution more informative than is required.
B Quality: Try to make your contribution one that is true.
    1 Do not say what you believe to be false.
    2 Do not say that for which you lack adequate evidence.
C Relation: Be relevant.
D Manner: Be perspicuous.
    1 Avoid obscurity of expression.
    2 Avoid ambiguity.

3 Be brief (avoid unnecessary prolixity).
4 Be orderly.

Sperber and Wilson (1986a: 36) point out that this formulation leaves many unanswered questions, including the source and nature of the Co-operative Principle and the maxims. Grice does not define what he means by expressions such as 'relevant' and 'perspicuous'. Moreover, he states that there might be more maxims than the already numerous ones listed above.

Grice used his principle and maxims to make the important claim that the speaker tries to meet certain standards in communication, and that the hearer uses these standards in deriving what the speaker intends to communicate. Grice gives an example of two people, A and B, having a conversation about a mutual friend C. A asks B how C is getting on in his new job, and B replies, 'Oh quite well, I think; he likes his colleagues, and he hasn't been to prison yet'. Grice comments, 'I think it is clear that whatever B implied, suggested, meant, etc., in this example, is distinct from what B said.' (1975: 43)

Grice (1975: 45) shifts the focus to those aspects of meaning which are not semantically determined. He calls these 'conversational implicature', as opposed to semantically determined 'conventional implicature'. Conversational implicature is worked out from the meaning of the sentence uttered, together with the context, on the basis of the assumption that communication is governed by the Co-operative Principle. The assumption is that the speaker has observed certain general maxims of communication.

For Grice, the crucial distinction between conventional implicature and conversational implicature is that the latter is calculable. Grice then proposes a formulation of how this calculation might be made:

(10) a He has said that p.
      b There is no reason to suppose that he is not observing the maxims, or at least their Co-operative Principle.
      c He could not be doing this unless he thought that q.
      d He knows (and knows that I know that he knows) that I can see that the supposition that he thinks that q is required.

21

  e He has done nothing to stop me thinking that q.
  f He intends me to think, or is at least willing to
     allow me to think, that q.
  g And so, he has implicated that q.

(Grice 1975: 50)

Sperber and Wilson maintain that this is not obviously a valid deductive argument. It is not clear which of (10a) to (10g) are meant to be premises and which conclusions. In (10c), the content of the implicature is introduced for the first time, but this can by no means be deduced from (10a) and (10b). Moreover, (10c) has to be either an independent premise itself, or derivable from (10a) and (10b) with some supplementary premises, which remain to be specified. In short, this does not offer an adequate account of the working out of conversational implicatures.

Neither semantic content nor Grice's general communication principles can help us to recover the conversational implicatures of the following utterance:

  (11) a She: Would you go and get some flowers?
        b He: I'm just going to Covent Garden.

If (11b) was used in a context containing assumption (12), then the utterance in (11b) would be treated as conveying proposition (13):

  (12) They sell flowers in Covent Garden.
  (13) He will be able to get some flowers.

On the other hand, if (11b) was used in a context containing assumption (14), then the utterance would be interpreted as communicating (15):

  (14) They do not sell flowers in Covent Garden.
  (15) He will not get any flowers.

RELEVANCE AND COGNITION

Relevance, according to Sperber and Wilson, is the key to human cognition. Their account of communication springs from the belief that the standards which govern inferential communication are based on the nature of human cognition. Humans pay attention to some phenomena rather than to others, and Sperber and Wilson's main claim is that humans tend to pay attention to those phenomena which are most relevant to them. The idea that new or newly presented information is processed in a context of existing assumptions is central to Sperber and Wilson's definition of relevance. To modify and improve a context is to have some effect on that context. They call this a *contextual effect* (1986a: 108). An utterance can have contextual effects in one of three ways. Sperber and Wilson (1990: 42–3) illustrate these three possibilities through the following examples.

The first form of contextual effect is *contextual implication*, that is further information which cannot be deduced from either existing assumptions or the new information alone. Suppose that one wakes up with the following thought:

(16) a If it's raining, I'll stay at home.

One looks out of the window and discovers:

(16) b It's raining.

From the existing assumption (16a) and the new information (16b), one can deduce some further information:

(16) c I'll stay at home.

The second form of contextual effect is the strengthening of existing assumptions. One wakes up, hearing what one thinks is a pattering on the roof, and forms the hypothesis:

(17) a It's raining.

One goes to the window, looks out, and discovers:

(17) b It *is* raining.

The third form of contextual effect is the contradiction and elimination of old assumptions. Assumptions placed in memory have varying degrees of strength. When two contradictory assumptions are derived, the weaker one is abandoned. Thus, one wakes up hearing what one thinks is a pattering on the roof, and forms the hypothesis:

(18) a It's raining.

One goes to the window and looks out. This time, however, one discovers that actually:

(18) b It's not raining, but there are cats on the roof.

Relevance is a matter of degree. In other words, the greater the contextual effects of a newly presented item of information, the more relevant it is. Consider the following examples:

(19) a If it rains, I'll stay at home.
      b It's raining.
      c It's raining and there are sodden leaves on the lawn.

In the context of (19a), which is artificially circumscribed, (19b) is intuitively more relevant than (19c). Yet (19b) and (19c) yield exactly the same contextual implication (19d), and thus have the same contextual effects in this context:

(19) d I'll stay at home.

It follows that the processing effort needed to derive contextual effects is crucial, and this leads to the notion of *optimal* relevance (Sperber and Wilson 1986a: 158). If processing effort were not taken into account, human beings would continue to process a newly received stimulus endlessly, combining it with an infinite stock of information, in an attempt to see if it might improve their representation of the world. Thus, it is optimal relevance which is sought, and not maximal relevance. As Sperber and Wilson put it, all the audience is entitled to expect is adequate effects for no unjustifiable effort. The most recent formulation of optimal relevance is as follows:

> An utterance, on a given interpretation, is optimally relevant if and only if:
>
> a) it achieves enough effects to be worthy of the hearer's attention;
> b) it puts the hearer to no gratuitous effort in achieving those effects.
>
> (Smith and Wilson 1992: 5)

This notion affects the earlier discussion of ostensive-inferential communication and ostensive behaviour, in that there is a significant difference between being exposed to an ostensive stimulus directed at oneself, and being exposed to other kinds of stimuli. Somebody who asks for your attention suggests that there is a good reason to assume that you might benefit from complying with his request. This suggestion may be made in bad faith, but it cannot be wholly ignored by the hearer. If a request is made, the speaker must have assumed that the hearer would have some motive for complying with it. Thus, if somebody shouts 'Watch out!' to you, you will react quite differently than if you were to overhear someone reading aloud 'Watch out!' in an adventure story. In short, in the case of an ostensive stimulus, the hearer can expect that the stimulus is intended to be relevant to her.

Sperber and Wilson thus argue that an act of ostensive communication automatically communicates what they call a *presumption of optimal relevance* (1986a: 158). In other words, in ostensive-inferential communication, the communicator necessarily communicates that the stimulus he uses is relevant to the audience. What is communicated, to the best of the communicator's knowledge, is that the ostensive stimulus is relevant enough to be worth the addressee's attention. Sperber and Wilson define the principle of relevance as follows:

> Every act of ostensive communication communicates the presumption of its own optimal relevance.
>
> (Sperber and Wilson 1986a: 158)

The fact that an ostensive stimulus creates an expectation of optimal relevance does not necessarily mean that it will actually be optimally relevant to the hearer. The speaker may be mistaken or he may be acting in bad faith. For example, I may say to you that they are showing *Richard II* at the nearby theatre and you may know that *Richard II* is no longer being played and that they are now showing *Richard III*. In this case, the information I have offered is irrelevant to you. However, it will still be appropriate and comprehensible as long as you can see how I might rationally have expected it to be optimally relevant to you. It will still be, as Smith and Wilson (1992: 6) put it, consistent with the principle of relevance, on the following grounds:

> Criterion of consistency with the principle of relevance:
> An utterance, on a given interpretation, is consistent with the principle of relevance if and only if the speaker might rationally have expected it to be optimally relevant to the hearer on that interpretation.

It is the consistency with the principle of relevance which acts as the sole criterion for evaluating alternative hypotheses about the intended interpretation of an utterance. An interpretation will be consistent with the principle of relevance as long as the speaker might rationally have expected the interpretation of his utterance to achieve an adequate range of contextual effects, while putting the hearer to no unjustifiable processing effort in achieving these effects. Sperber and Wilson's claim is that the criterion of consistency with the principle of relevance provides an adequate explanation of the role of contextual assumptions in all aspects of utterance interpretation.

The responsibility for successful communication is not shared equally by the communicator and the addressee. It is left to the communicator to make correct assumptions about the codes and contextual information that the addressee will have accessible and will be likely to use in the comprehension process. The responsibility for avoiding misunderstanding also lies with the communicator. All that the addressee has to do is to recover the interpretation which is consistent with the principle of relevance.

IMPLICATURES

An utterance communicates a range of assumptions, but only some are intended by the speaker. Others are accidental. Thus the hearer might recover assumptions about the speaker from his Welsh accent, without his intending to communicate them. Or a speaker might have a nasal voice which indicates that he has a cold, but without his intending to do so. The hearer is induced to derive some cognitive effects, without the speaker making manifest that he intends to communicate them. These stimuli fall outside the realm of ostensive communication. In other cases, the speaker intends to communicate certain assumptions, but does not intend to publicise his intention to do so. This is considered in the discussion of covert communication in Chapter 3.

Among those assumptions which the speaker communicates overtly (that is ostensively), some are communicated explicitly and others implicitly. An assumption obtained by the development of the logical forms encoded by an utterance is called an *explicature* (Sperber and Wilson 1986a: 182). In contrast, assumptions which are derivable from the proposition expressed by the utterance together with the context are called *implicatures*. The notion of implicature was first used by Grice (1975), but this distinction between explicature and implicature does not correspond to Grice's distinction between 'saying' and 'implicating' (Sperber and Wilson 1986a, 1995, Carston 1988b, Blakemore 1992). Sperber and Wilson (1986a: 195) argue that both the contextual assumption and the conclusion are implications of the utterance, and call the former an implicated premise and the latter implicated conclusion.

Some implicatures are strongly backed by the speaker, as in the following example:

(20) a Kay: What do you do in your leisure time?
      b Paul: I went to Glyndebourne last Saturday.

The explicatures of (20b) include the following assumption:

(21) Paul has said that he went to Glyndebourne on the previous Saturday.

Utterence (21) does not directly answer the question in (20a). However, it does give Kay immediate access to her encyclopaedic knowledge about Glyndebourne, which includes contextual assumption (22):

(22) One goes to Glyndebourne to watch a performance of the opera.

If processed in a context containing (22), (20b) would yield (23):

(23) Paul went to the opera at Glyndebourne.

It is not difficult to see that Kay is expected by Paul to process (20b) in a context which contains (23) and derive (24):

(24) Paul likes going to the opera in his leisure time.

It can be said that Paul has strongly implicated (24) by saying (20b). Thus Paul intends both the contextual assumptions (22) and (23) and the conclusion (24) to be recovered by Kay.

Other implicatures are very weakly backed by the speaker. In the case of these weak implicatures, the hearer has to take on a great responsibility if she is to believe them. When (20b) gives Kay access to her encyclopaedic information about Glyndebourne, she may retrieve information other than (24). For example, Kay may supply (25) and (26) and derive (27) and (28):

(25) People who like to spend their leisure time in going to the opera are cultured.

(26) People who are cultured like going to art galleries, concerts and theatres.

(27) Paul is cultured.

(28) Paul likes going to art galleries, concerts and theatres.

The communicator can achieve successful communication through weak implicatures. The indirect answer in (20b) offers a range of possible interpretations, which would not be available if the answer had been direct. By choosing an indirect answer, Paul must have expected some of these interpretations to bring contextual effects to outweigh the extra processing effort involved. That is to say that, however weakly communicated they may be, Paul has overtly communicated (27) and (28). He does not strongly back them and Kay takes the responsibility to a degree for supplying these particular premises and conclusions. In other circumstances, where his social status was in question, Paul could have expected Kay to supply just these premises and conclusion. The speaker has no way of making sure of his success in communication. However, he can correctly assume that his addressee is likely to access and use certain assumptions in interpreting his utterance. He can thus aim at a high probability of success.

The question then arises as to how far Kay should seek for possibilities. In other words, how long should she keep adding premises to the context and recovering further conclusions? She could add (29) to the context and derive (30):

(29) People who go to Glyndebourne do not like hunting, shooting and fishing.

(30) Paul does not like hunting, shooting and fishing.

It is not easy to say whether Paul has given Kay any encouragement to supply the premise in (29) and derive (30).

From the hearer's point of view, there are two criteria which she uses in deciding how far she is to investigate. Firstly, in deciding what has been communicated, she uses the criterion of consistency with the principle of relevance. Secondly, in deciding how far she should continue providing premises, adding them to the context, and deriving conclusions on her own responsibility, she uses the criterion governing her own cognitive activities, namely, the search for maximal relevance. That is, she goes as far as she finds it relevant to go. She would not go beyond the point where her processing effort outweighs the effects she achieves from the derived conclusions. If the effect obtained from the derived assumptions is weighed against processing effort, there will be a point at which it is not worth going any further.

The conclusion to be drawn from this example is that there is no clear cut-off point between assumptions strongly backed by the communicator, and assumptions derived from the utterance on the addressee's sole responsibility. It can be argued in the example above that (23) is a strongly implicated premise and (24) a strongly implicated conclusion, which are strongly backed by the speaker. In contrast, (25) and (26) are weakly implicated premises and (27) and (28) weakly implicated conclusions. Though there is some backing from the speaker, the backing is weak, and the hearer has to derive them on her own responsibility. Nevertheless, both strong and weak implicatures are ostensively communicated, and therefore both are consistent with the principle of relevance.

However weakly communicated they may be, weak implicatures comply with the requirement of overtness, which is crucial to ostensive communication. They must be distinguished from forms of covert communication, which are non-ostensive and therefore do not exhibit this overtness. In this framework, communicating an impression is defined as relatively minor alterations in the manifestness of a large number of assumptions, instead of major alterations of a few assumptions (Sperber and Wilson 1986a: 59).

THE DETERMINATION OF CONTEXT

It was suggested in Chapter 1 that the lack of an adequate account of the nature and role of context has been a fundamental weakness in writings on the language of advertising, and in the theories of communication on which they are based. A commonly held assumption is that the context for the comprehension of an utterance is given, so that the hearer combines the newly presented information with the context which is already present in her mind at the beginning of communication. The context is predetermined, the utterance is made, the interpretation process takes place, and, lastly, the utterance's relevance is assessed. In effect, relevance is regarded as a by-product of the comprehension process.

Sperber and Wilson argue that this is highly implausible. In the first place, any of the hearer's assumptions could be used in the interpretation of an utterance. Moreover, human beings are not in the business of simply assessing the relevance of new information. Their interest is to identify the information and process it as efficiently as possible. The assessment of relevance is not the goal of the comprehension process, but rather a means to the end of comprehension.

Sperber and Wilson therefore contend that the selection of an adequate context is a vital part of the interpretation process, which must be accounted for by pragmatic theory. The hearer of an utterance has available a set of potential contexts, from which an actual context needs to be chosen. A context consists of assumptions drawn from different sources, such as long-term memory, short-term memory, and perception. This does not mean that any arbitrary subset of the total set of assumptions available might become a context. Sperber and Wilson claim (1986a: 138) that the organisation of the hearer's encyclopaedic memory, and the mental activity in which she is engaged, limit the class of potential contexts from which an actual context can be chosen at any given time.

The nature of context can be illustrated as follows. Let us assume that there is a small immediately accessible context, fixed in advance, consisting of the proposition which has most recently been processed, together with its contextual implications, and any assumptions used in deriving these contextual implications. When new information is received, it will be processed in this immediate context. In the following examples, some degree of relevance is immediately achieved if the initial context is (31) and the proposition expressed by the utterance is (32):

(31) If the opera is by Mozart, Peter will go.
(32) The opera is by Mozart.

But if the proposition expressed is (33a), (33b) or (33c), the results are different:

(33) a The opera is by the composer whom you have just mentioned.
　　 b The opera is *The Magic Flute*.

c The opera is this (the music which is being played at the time of the utterance).

Unless the initial context is extended in some way, no degree of relevance can be achieved in the cases of (33a) to (33c). If the goal of processing is to find an interpretation consistent with the principle of relevance, the hearer will be forced to add further information to the initial context (31). This information will be remembered from earlier exchanges, as in the case of (33a), or recovered from encyclopaedic memory, as in the case of (33b), or derived from perception, as in the case of (33c). Thus the accessibility of potential contexts is partly determined by the content of the proposition being processed. The goal will be to find premises which will combine with the old assumptions and yield adequate contextual implications in return for minimal processing effort.

There are practical rather than theoretical limitations to the extent of the processing effort. The number and complexity of extensions involved for communication to be successful will be limited by the hearer's capacity for extending the context, and by the constraints on the effort side of comprehension. But there is no other restriction on the number of extensions that may be used to establish the relevance of a given proposition.

Furthermore, the speaker can actually direct his hearer towards an appropriate context, given that he holds specific expectations about how his utterance will be relevant. This process is illustrated by the following example:

(34) a Kay: Would you like to go to *Tosca*?
b Paul: I'm not keen on Puccini.

Paul has not answered Kay's question directly, but he has implied an answer. Kay has to recover the intended effects of the utterance. She must supply certain premises, either by retrieving them from her memory or by deriving them in some way from what she knows. The criterion of consistency with the principle of relevance provides her with an adequate guide. One of the premises which Kay should be able to supply is:

(35) *Tosca* was composed by Puccini.

By processing Paul's reply (34b) against a context which contains assumption (35), Kay should derive the contextual implication (36):

(36) Paul would not like to go to *Tosca*.

This example demonstrates that mutual knowledge is not a prerequisite for successful communication. Even if Kay did not possess the information in (35) prior to the exchange in (34), she may come to acquire (35) as a result of the exchange. All she has to do is to supply premises which a rational speaker might have thought would lead to an interpretation which is optimally relevant. Similarly, Paul does not need to know if Kay already has the information in (35). She would be expected to come to have this knowledge as a result of interpreting his utterance. By applying the criterion of consistency with the principle of relevance, she would have to supply premise (35) and then deduce conclusion (36). Paul may expect Kay to supply this premise, not because he has ground for thinking that it is already highly accessible to her, but rather because his utterance has made it accessible to her. In other words, by producing the implicit answer (34b), he has constrained her choice of context and directed her towards a particular interpretation.

LOOSE TALK

An utterance has traditionally been regarded as a description of a state of affairs, a definition which raises considerable problems. In this view, the speaker of an utterance commits himself to the truth of the proposition expressed by that utterance. For example, supposing that (37) was said by Paul on 7 December 1992, it can be said that the speaker of (37) commits himself to the truth of (38):

(37) I went to church yesterday.
(38) Paul went to church on the 6th of December 1992.

However, this analysis clearly does not apply in such cases as imperatives and interrogatives (Wilson and Sperber 1988a). Nor does it apply to linguistic devices much used in advertising, such as metaphor (Wilson and Sperber 1988b).

Sperber and Wilson (1986a: 228–9) argue that an utterance can be used not only to represent a state of affairs in the world, but also to represent another utterance it resembles in content. They go on to say that every utterance is a representation of the thought the speaker intends to communicate. If I say to somebody 'You're a pig!', I am not using the utterance as a description of a state of affairs, but as a faithful representation of a thought which I intend to communicate, with metaphorical effect.

Moreover, Wilson and Sperber (1988b: 137) argue that it is the 'faithfulness' of the proposition expressed by the utterance to the thought expressed which is at stake. By 'faithfulness', they mean that an utterance resembles another one closely enough in relevant respects. The introduction of this notion stems from the problems which emerge from the maxim of truthfulness. Consider the following exchange:

(39) a Kay: What did John Major say about Iraqgate?
     b Paul: 'I didn't know anything about it'.

Reported speech presents problems for a framework which employs the maxim of truthfulness, for the speaker of (39b) does not guarantee the truth of the proposition expressed by it. Wilson and Sperber (1988b: 139) argue that reports of speech, like any other utterance, come with a guarantee of faithfulness. Moreover, faithfulness is a matter of degree, for the utterance can be more or less faithful to the original. Thus (39b) may be very close to what Major actually said, or it may be a rough summary of what he said. In either case, between the propositions expressed by the prime minister's utterance and Paul's utterance in (39b) there is a resemblance in content, or, more technically, in logical and contextual implications.

Thus, according to Sperber and Wilson (1986a: 228–9), an utterance can be used to represent things in two ways. On the one hand, it can be used to represent a state of affairs, in virtue of being a true description of that state of affairs. This they call *descriptive use*. On the other hand, an utterance can represent another utterance in virtue of some resemblance in content, in that they share logical and contextual implications. They talk about this as *interpretive use* or *interpretive resemblance*.

Interpretive resemblance is context-dependent. Consider the following exchange:

(40) a Kay: How much do you earn?
     b Paul: I earn £24,000 a year.

Supposing Paul in fact earns £23,744.63 a year, a descriptive use of (40b) would be false, strictly speaking. However, an utterance does not have to be true to be appropriate. If this exchange took place in a context of casual conversation between acquaintances, the speaker, who aims to achieve optimal relevance, would judge it to be appropriate to use (40b). It would yield the same contextual effects in terms of assumptions about Paul's spending power and standard of living. Moreover, (40b) would not cause the hearer the extra processing effort which the precise answer (41) would involve:

(41) I earn £23,744.63 a year

But if Kay was Paul's accountant, filling in his tax returns at a time when the border between paying tax at 25 per cent and 40 per cent was £23,800 a year, (40b) would not be acceptable, for it would not result in appropriate assumptions about levels of tax and tax allowances. The exact answer (41) would be required in this case.

The fact that interpretive resemblance is a matter of degree gives rise to the notion of *loose talk*, which is crucial to the analysis of metaphor and images of women in advertising in Chapters 5 and 6 respectively. At one end of the scale, when the proposition expressed by an utterance is identical with the thought it represents, the utterance is described as 'literal' (Sperber and Wilson 1986a: 231) At the other end of the scale, when the proposition expressed by an utterance and the thought it represents share no content, there would be no resemblance and the utterance would be unacceptable. But when the proposition expressed by an utterance resembles the thought it represents only to some degree, Sperber and Wilson (1986a: 234) call the utterance *loose*.

They argue that a loose use of language is rife in ordinary communication, and that strictly literal use is rare. Utterances create expectations of optimal relevance, rather than literal truth. Often the most economical means of communicating the speaker's thought is to speak not literally but loosely. From the hearer's point of view, unless there is a specific reason to believe that the utterance is literal, it should be assumed that there is some degree of looseness in the utterance.

This matches our intuitions. For example, I once lived in a flat which was located exactly opposite the main façade of the British Museum. All my visitors were informed of this fact in advance, in addition to being provided with my address. However, every single one of them used to point out on their arrival, with a tone of surprise, that my flat was exactly opposite the British Museum.

CONCLUSION

Sperber and Wilson's Relevance Theory thus provides the most comprehensive account of utterance interpretation. Their framework is based on ostention, the communicator's intention to communicate and to publicise his intention, and the principle that an ostentive stimulus creates a presumption of optimal relevance. The task of the audience in ostensive communication is to process the communicator's utterance against background information and derive an interpretation which is consistent with the principle of relevance. Relevance Theory will now be applied to the analysis of advertisements, focusing on covert communication, puns, metaphors, and images of women in advertising.

Since the publication of the hardback edition of this book, Sperber and Wilson have brought out a second edition of *Relevance*. Although the revisions do not affect the way the theory works as explained in this chapter, one of them needs to be mentioned, since it affects one of the definitions cited here. Thus, according to Sperber and Wilson (1995: 260), there are two principles of relevance, defined as follows:

1 Human cognition tends to be geared to the maximisation of relevance.
2 Every act of ostensive communication communicates a presumption of its own optimal relevance.

The first principle is to do with cognition, while the second one is about communication. The second principle is identical to the principle of relevance originally set out in the 1986 edition, and Sperber and Wilson continue to refer to the second one as the principle of relevance. The change is, as they put it, 'expository and not substantive' (Sperber and Wilson 1995: 261).

3

COVERT
COMMUNICATION

INTRODUCTION

This chapter investigates how advertisers seek to achieve their primary goal of persuading or influencing an audience. Crystal and Davy (1983: 222) state that there are two main functions of advertising: informing and persuading. The latter of these Corke (1986: 15) calls influencing. However, these two functions are not of equal importance, in that information is subordinated to persuasion (Packard 1981; Pearson and Turner 1966). The advertiser does not inform for the sake of improving his addressee's knowledge of the world, but only to sell a product. He would be quite content if he could manage to persuade his audience to buy his product, while failing to inform them of anything at all. In contrast, he would not have succeeded in his task if he provided a great deal of information but failed to persuade anybody to buy his product. Needless to say, this only applies to commercial advertising, the focus of all that follows, and not to public benefit advertising.

'Covert communication' is a response to inter-related problems which advertisers face in their task of persuading or influencing. They wish to avoid negative social reactions, which may arise in response to certain aspects of their advertisements, such as the use of sex and the exploitation of the notion of snobbery. These problematic elements in their advertisements appear to boost sales, so that advertisers want to continue to use them, but they simultaneously wish to avoid taking any responsibility for so doing. This problem is compounded by the low level of trust and social co-operation existing between advertisers and their audience, which enhances the possibility of negative social reactions emanating from the public. At the same time, lack of trust makes it harder for advertisers to convince an audience that a product is really all that it is claimed to be.

TRUST AND SOCIAL CO-OPERATION IN OSTENSIVE COMMUNICATION

One advantage of engaging in ostensive communication, across a wide range of circumstances, is that it may encourage the fixation of belief. If the speaker's intention to inform his hearer of something is recognised by the hearer, this can help make her believe it. Sperber and Wilson (1986a: 21–2) give the following example:

> Suppose that Mary intends to please Peter. If Peter becomes aware of her intention to please him, this may in itself be enough to please him. Similarly, when the inmates of a prison recognise their warden's intention to make them fear him, this may be enough in itself to make them fear him. There is one type of intention for which this possibility, rather than being exceptional, is regularly exploited: intentions to inform are quite generally fulfilled by being made recognisable.

Sperber and Wilson state that it is not difficult to see why making the speaker's intention to inform something overt may help him succeed in making his hearer believe it: 'the realisation that a trustworthy communicator intends to make you believe something is an excellent reason for believing it' (Sperber and Wilson 1986a: 163).

However, lack of trust does not prevent ostensive communication from taking place. The success of ostensive communication is defined as the hearer recovering the speaker's informative intention, not as the speaker making the hearer believe something. It is possible for the hearer successfully to recover the set of assumptions intended by the speaker without actually believing them.

Moreover, trust is not in itself necessary for belief to occur. If there is trust between the speaker and hearer, it will be just an extra contextual assumption and it will help the hearer believe what the speaker communicates. But it is possible for a belief to be formed without trust between them.

Co-operation at the cognitive level is the essential prerequisite for ostensive communication, not co-operation at the social level. If Serbia declares war on Albania, the Albanian government pays attention to this stimulus, processes it, understands it, and acts on it. Cognitive co-operation is successfully achieved, even if a breakdown in social co-operation results. Ostensive communication has taken place, albeit in the framework of hostile social relations.

Communication takes place in situations marked by varying degrees of trust and social co-operation. A happily married couple exemplifies a social situation where a trustworthy speaker communicates with a trusting addressee. Together they strive to maximise the relevance of all new information in order to improve their knowledge of the world. The husband can rely on his wife to believe something which he intends to make her believe, and vice versa. But it would be highly unrealistic to assume that communication always takes place in such a situation. A prison warder is in a position to make an inmate's life difficult, and for a prisoner to believe this fact it is sufficient that she should know about the warder's power. But if the warder says 'I'll be nice to you', the inmate has few reasons to believe this statement. Prisoners are not trusting addressees.

The 'strength' with which a communicated assumption is entertained is commensurate with the hearer's trust in the speaker. In this example, Peter says to Mary:

(1) I'll make you a meal because you're tired.

If Mary does not trust him, she will not believe (1). If she trusts him a little, she will believe (1) a little. If she has great trust in him, she will believe (1) to the extent which Peter intended. This said, Peter might not only satisfy Mary's expectations, but he might also exploit her trust.

Messages which are indirectly and weakly communicated in situations characterised by low levels of trust are nevertheless ostensively communicated. In the following case, the speaker takes advantage of the fact that he communicated certain assumptions by implicature, rather than explicature, and then denies his backing for these assumptions. Malcolm Turnbull, acting for Peter Wright in the *Spycatcher* trial, referred to a letter written by Sir Robert Armstrong, a senior civil servant, to the chair of a firm of publishers. The letter communicated the following:

> (2) The government did not have a copy of *Their Trade is Treachery*.

Armstrong agreed under questioning that the government had in reality obtained page proofs of the book in question some six weeks before the letter had been written. This was followed by the famous exchange:

> T: I put it to you that this letter contains an untruth.
> A: It does not say that we have already got a copy of the book, that is quite true.
> T: So it contains a lie?
> A: As one person said, it is perhaps being economical with the truth.
>
> (Edited extracts from 'The wily colonial boy versus the upper class Brit', *The Sunday Times*, 15 March 1987. 'T' stands for Turnbull and 'A' for Armstrong.)

Armstrong had originally intended to communicate (2), even though it was by implicature and in a weak form. But (2) was nevertheless ostensively communicated, for Armstrong made his informative intention mutually manifest to the publisher and to himself.

Cases of limited or non-existent trust in ostensive communication are not exceptional, and may even be the norm. They are rife in political debate, legal argument, academic discussion, and commercial bargaining. Let us suppose that (3) was said by a double-glazing salesman to a potential customer:

> (3) You would find it good value for money.

The customer would not regard it as a sufficient reason to believe (3) that the salesman intended to make her believe this statement. It is mutually manifest that he would be likely to say (3), even if his statement were to be inconsistent with the truth. The statement is not truly worth the hearer's while to believe, because the double-glazing salesman and his customer are unequal interlocutors. Since the customer does not regard the salesman as trustworthy, the salesman has to aim to achieve his intended effects by means of an artfully crafted stimulus, and not by means of the customer's trusting disposition toward him. He cannot afford to rely on the addressee's co-operation at the social level.

Not surprisingly, advertising is typical of a situation in which the speaker is not trustworthy and the hearer is not trusting. It is mutually manifest to both the advertiser and his addressee that the advertiser is saying something because he wants her to buy a product or service. The advertiser's task is to make her believe something about a product without her trusting in him, or, indeed, despite her distrusting him. This leads to a variety of strategies on the part of the advertiser. Covert communication is one of these strategies, and others are explored in subsequent chapters.

ADVANTAGES OF ENGAGING IN COVERT COMMUNICATION

When the speaker's informative intention is not made mutually manifest, Sperber and Wilson argue that genuine ostensive, or overt, communication does not occur. They illustrate this by the following non-verbal example of non-ostensive communication:

> Suppose, for instance, that Mary wants Peter to mend her broken hair-drier, but does not want to ask him openly. What she does is begin to take her hair-drier to pieces and leave the pieces lying around as if she were in the process of mending it. She does not expect Peter to be taken in by this staging; in fact, if he really believed that she was in the process of mending her hair-drier herself, he would probably not interfere. She does expect him to be clever enough to work out that this is a staging intended to inform him of the fact that she needs some help with her hair-drier. However, she does not expect him to reason along just these lines. Since she is not really asking, if Peter fails to help, it will not really count as a refusal either.
>
> (Sperber and Wilson 1986a: 30)

Sperber and Wilson (1986a: 30) state that this example is not a case of ostensive communication, but rather a 'covert form of information transmission'. There is 'an intuitive reluctance to say that Mary *meant* that she wanted Peter's help, or that she was *communicating* with Peter in the sense we are trying to

40

characterise' (their italics). This reluctance is 'well-founded', since Mary's second-order intention to have her first-order informative intention recognised has been hidden from Peter.

Bencherif and Tanaka (1987) have used the notion of covert information transmission as a basis on which to elaborate the idea of 'covert communication'. They sum up the difference between ostensive and covert communication as follows:

> *Ostensive communication*: an overt form of communication where there is, on the part of the speaker, an intention to alter the mutual cognitive environment of the speaker and the hearer.

> *Covert communication*: a case of communication where the intention of the speaker is to alter the cognitive environment of the hearer, i.e. to make a set of assumptions more manifest to her, without making this intention mutually manifest.

The notions of informative intention and communicative intention in Relevance Theory are crucial here. In covert communication, the speaker intends to achieve the fulfilment of his informative intention without the aid of communicative intention. In contrast to what happens in ostensive communication, he does not intend to make his informative intention mutually manifest to the addressee and himself. He does intend to affect the cognitive environment of his addressee by making her recover certain assumptions, but he avoids the modification of the mutual cognitive environment of the addressee and himself by not making this intention mutually manifest. In other words, he does not publicise his informative intention.

In covert communication, the hearer does not have the speaker's guarantee of optimal relevance to guide her, but other stimuli can be used to overcome this deficiency. The communicator relies on the addressee noticing certain non-linguistic stimuli, given the way in which her general cognitive system is organised. Sex and food are typical stimuli which draw the audience's attention. Sperber and Wilson (1986a: 151–5) argue that this is because human beings are more susceptible to some cognitive phenomena than to others, as cognition is designed to pick out relevant phenomena and process them in the most efficient way. Sometimes attention is 'wired into' our perceptual system, as with bright lights and loud noises. At other times it is learned . The notion of relevance is thus valid not only in ostensive-inferential communication, but also in determining which non-linguistic stimuli are likely to be processed, and in what way.

The hearer often does not get her reward entirely through inference in covert communication, for the speaker exploits the fact that humans get a kind of pleasure out of processing certain stimuli. Advertisers, for example, include illustrations to compensate the addressee for her attention. The illustration may have nothing to do with the advertiser's overt message, and may simply serve as a 'reward' for her attention (Cook 1992: 225). Advertisers even carry out research to test the degree of sexual arousal accompanying certain campaigns (Packard 1981: 221).

The hearer also has to take a larger share of the responsibility in recovering the speaker's meaning than in overtly communicated messages. One advantage for the speaker, especially in social situations where trust and co-operation between interlocutors are limited or lacking, is that the hearer becomes more involved in the process of communication (Williamson 1983: 167). Even in overt communication, speakers in such situations often rely on implicatures rather than explicatures, or on weak communication, which similarly require greater responsibility on the part of the hearer.

Going one step further, a major advantage of covert communication is that it enables the speaker to avoid accepting responsibility for social consequences which might result from overt communication of the information. Modifying the mutual cognitive environment of the communicator and the addressee could bring with it certain social implications, which could be embarrassing or harmful for the communicator. The speaker still wishes to make certain assumptions manifest to the hearer, but he does not want to be held responsible for having done so.

In contrast, the speaker in ostensive communication leaves the fulfilment of his informative intention 'in the hands of' the addressee, by making his informative intention mutually manifest (Sperber and Wilson: 1986a: 62). The addressee may accept his message or reject it, and it is here that trust and co-operation are important. But either way, the social relationship between communicator and addressee will have been affected. As Sperber and Wilson (1986a: 61–2) put it:

Mutual manifestness may be of little cognitive importance, but it is of crucial social importance. A change in the mutual cognitive environment of two people is a change in their possibility of interaction.

Another social situation calling for covert communication refers back to the problem of trust and co-operation noted above. The speaker does not publicise his informative intention when he believes that revealing it would have an adverse effect on its fulfilment. Thus, if Paul is trying to impress Kay, the realisation that Paul intends to make her believe something good about himself would not be a good reason for Kay to believe it. On the contrary, it is likely that it would prove to be an excellent reason for her not to believe it. In the same way, an advertiser would not be likely to get very far with the following caption, unless he somehow managed to turn it into a self-mocking parody:

(4) I want you to buy large amounts of this product so that both I and the manufacturer can make big profits.

COVERT COMMUNICATION IN ADVERTISING

In advertising, covert communication is employed for two main puposes. At a very general level, there is a constant tendency for the advertiser to try to make the addressee forget that he is trying to sell her something:

Some advertisers may seek to stretch the credibility of their advertisement by plagiarizing the 'house style' of the magazine. Agency personnel I interviewed believed that this approach could make advertisements immediately accessible and appealing, especially to the younger audience. It is one way of seducing readers into paying attention to advertisements which they might otherwise selectively avoid.

(Myers 1983: 211)

In this type of covert communication, the advertiser intends to communicate something to his audience, without making mutually manifest the identity of the speaker. However, there is some controversy as to whether this kind of tactic is truly effective. According to Myers, some agencies 'despised this approach, not because they considered it underhand, but because they felt it lacked distinction and impact' (Myers 1983: 211).

The second purpose of covert communication, on which this chapter focuses, is to avoid taking responsibility for the social consequences of certain implications arising from advertisements. Thus, covert communication in advertising is often found in cases involving sexual interpretations, which may be related to subliminal aspects of sexuality in advertising (Key 1973; Packard 1981: 75–85). The following caption for a Haig Whisky advertisement in Japan (Kleinman 1984) is a good illustration of this kind of covert communication:

(5) *O-shigoto   yori   mo   oishii   koto.*
HON-work   than   even   delicious   thing

Something that is even more delicious than work.

The illustration shows a young woman and a bottle of Haig whisky. The honorific prefix *o* is markedly feminine, so that the phrase in the caption appears to be uttered by the woman in the picture. Considering that it is an advertisement for whisky, the audience should recover (6):

(6) Haig whisky is more delicious than work.

However, the word *koto* in (5) means 'thing or event', and the word *mono*, meaning 'thing or object', would at first sight have been more appropriate. The girl in the illustration is pretty, heavily made-up, and is wearing a low-cut top. Kleinman (1984) makes the following comment on this advertisement:

> The sexual innuendo is unmistakable. In the West the feminists lobby would be outraged. But the picture is pretty.

The audience will thus be encouraged to derive (7):

(7) Sex with me is more delicious than work.

The advertiser may have intended his audience to recover both (6) and (7), but he did not ostensively communicate both of them. In the case of (7), it cannot be said that the advertiser intended it to be manifest on the basis of making this informative intention mutually manifest. Certainly, the advertiser deliberately chose to use the word *koto* (thing/event), but this is not enough to argue that he ostensively refers to sex. He could claim that he meant to communicate (8):

(8) Drinking Haig whisky is more delicious than work.

In this case the use of the word *koto* would emphasise the act of drinking. The advertiser conveys (7) covertly, leaving himself room to deny any intention to communicate the sexual innuendo. The feminist lobby in Japan is said to be weak (Condon 1991: 59), but if the advertiser were to depict a young woman ostensively saying (7), it might nevertheless antagonise a considerable number of women. The advertiser therefore does not make his informative intention to transmit assumptions about sex mutually manifest, because of the possible social consequences of doing so. The recovery of his informative intention by his audience is not helped by the fact that he obscures it. However, the picture of the girl in her provocative dress is sufficient to help the audience to get the message.

It is not only women who are treated in this way. The following caption from a Japanese advertisement for men's toiletries is accompanied by an illustration showing the face and torso of a young Western man with long hair (arms not shown):

(9) *Otoko wa   seinoo.*
    man   TOP capacity

For a man, it is capacity (which is desirable).

Considering that it is an advertisement, the following premise must be added to the context:

(10) The product advertised helps the buyer to attain what is desirable.

When assumptions (9) and (10) are combined, the following conclusion can be recovered by the audience:

(11) The product helps the buyer to attain his capacity.

The sexual innuendo turns on the word *seinoo* (capacity). This refers to functional capacity and is usually employed to describe machines or electrical equipment. It is not common to use the word to describe people. However, the brand name, Tech 21, has overtones of technology, and it may be the company's principle to advertise the product in association with machinery. Perhaps it is not just women who are treated as sex machines in advertising.

There is a further possible interpretation of the caption. Two Chinese characters are combined to transcribe *seinoo*. Each of these has its own meaning if it occurs independently, that is, *sei* (sex) and *noo* (ability). Thus, the following interpretation is possible:

(12) *Otoko wa sei noo.*
man TOP sex ability

For a man, it is sexual ability (which is desirable).

This interpretation is reinforced by the illustration of a man's naked torso, with overtones of a picture from a gay magazine. When (12) is processed in a context which contains assumptions (10) and (11), the following conclusion will be recovered:

(13) The product helps the buyer attain his sexual ability.

It can hardly be argued that the advertiser has overtly communicated (12) and (13) by making mutually manifest his intention to do so. *Seinoo* (capacity) is a single word, even though it is written with two separate Chinese characters. There is no obvious justification for breaking it down and considering the meaning of each character separately, especially as characters can be employed in Japanese for purely phonetic purposes.

The reasons for employing covert communication in this example are fairly clear. An advertiser promoting men's toiletries could stand to gain considerable advantages from associating his product with enhanced sexual performance, but an explicit association with sexuality might be regarded as vulgar and distasteful. In Japan's men's toiletries are often purchased by wives as a gift for their husbands, and such women might be put off by an overt association between toiletries and sexual ability. The advertiser might even be accused of encouraging homosexuality, a taboo subject in Japanese society. The advertiser thus intends to inform his audience of assumptions about sex, but wishes to avoid the unwelcome social consequences which might spring from making this intention mutually manifest. He hopes that the audience will be able to recover these assumptions on their own responsibility, with a little help from the illustration.

One might expect sex to be covertly exploited in advertising spirits and toiletries, but it is by no means limited to these categories

(Packard 1981: 236–7; Pearson and Turner 1966: 58). Even miniature television sets are not exempt from this kind of treatment. Consider the following example (see Plates 3.1 and 3.2 respectively):

(14) Mi-tai   mono o   gamansuru   to
     watch-want to thing ACC   forbear   if

     ningen   ga   chijimimasu.
     personality   NOM   shrunk

     If you go without watching what you want to watch, your personality will shrink.

(15) Mi-tai   mono o   gamansuru to jinsei
     watch-want   thing ACC   forbear   if life

     kuraku   narimasu.
     depressing   become

     If you go without watching what you want to watch, your life will be depressing.

These captions are accompanied by similar illustrations. Three young Western people accompany (14). Two girls dominate the picture, holding each other intimately. A boy holds one of the girls from behind with one hand, and he has a miniature television set in the other. There is a faint suggestion of an orgy. Caption (15) is illustrated by two Western girls, intimately close to one another, with one girl holding the other from behind. The girl who is held is playing the piano, on the keys of which is placed a miniature television set. There are strong overtones of a lesbian relationship, and a sense of forbidden romance.

Some text attached to these captions reinforces these associations. (16) and (17) accompany (14) and (15), respectively (my translation):

(16) *Jinrui hatten no rekishi, kore sunawachi kookishin juusoku no rekishi. 'Are mo mitai, kore mo mitai' no yajiuma-konjoo koso, ningen-seichoo no gendooryoku nano de arimasu . . .*

The history of the development of mankind is precisely the history of the satisfaction of curiosity. 'Want to see this. Want to see that . . .' The curiosity which drives a mob is the source of energy which has driven mankind to grow this far . . .

(17) *Are-kore to, mamanaranu-koto no ooi kono yononaka. Semete, mi-tai mono gurai jiyuu ni mire-nakya, nani ga*

Plate 3.1 Epson (14)

Plate 3.2 Epson (15)

tanoshimi de ikite-iru no ka wakara-naku narimasu yo ne . . .

Can't do this, can't do that . . . There are many things forbidden in this world. What's the point of living unless we can at least watch what we want to when we want to . . .?

Caption and text are closely related. (14) and (16) both encourage curiosity: (14) says that if you give up your curiosity you will 'shrink', while (16) says that it is curiosity which helps people to grow. There is a contrast between *chijimu* (shrink) and *seichoo* (growth). The word *chijimu* (shrink) is normally used to describe an inanimate object, and it is unusual for people to be said to 'shrink'. The word hints at the lack of an erection. Thus, (14) may be interpreted as follows:

(18) If you refrain from watching what you want to watch, your penis will shrink.

To the extent that the illustration suggests an orgy, it could also be interpreted as:

(19) If you refrain from having an orgy, your penis will shrink.

Both (15) and (17) are about taboos: (15) says that life is depressing when one goes without the forbidden, and (17) asks what is the point of living if we are to go without what is forbidden. With the illustration suggesting a lesbian relationship, the following interpretation is thus possible:

(20) If you go without a lesbian relationship, your life will be depressing.

There is another caption, in English, accompanying both advertisements, and it pushes the interpretation in the same sort of direction:

(21) Anytime OK! Everywhere OK!

What it is which is all right at any time and everywhere is ambivalent. Considering that this is an advertisement for a miniature television set and that the original caption is apparently talking about not being able to watch something, the following interpretation is possible:

(22) With our television set you can watch television anywhere at any time.

But in a context in which (21) is present with (19) or (20), it is
possible to recover (23) and (24):

(23) You can have an orgy anywhere at any time.

(24) You can have lesbian sex anywhere at any time.

There is an intuitive reluctance to say that the advertiser has
overtly communicated these sexual interpretations. They appear
irrelevant to advertisements for a miniature television set. There
seems to be no reason why the advertiser should encourage an orgy
or a lesbian relationship, which are taboo in Japanese society. Sex is
indeed used in advertising in order to catch and retain attention, but
such a discussion goes onto a 'subliminal' level (Key 1973; Packard
1981: 75–85), which is beyond the concerns of this book.

The decision to engage in this form of covert communication
in these television advertisements may have been related to
where they appeared. They both appeared in a Japanese magazine *Fookasu* (Focus) (22 February 1985 and 22 March 1985), a
publication akin to the supplement to the *News of the World* in
Britain. *Fookasu* carries much 'racy' material, and the advertiser
seems to have calculated that his advertisements would not be
too offensive to such an audience. However, he is still careful
not to make his informative intention mutually manifest and not
to take the entire responsibility for such interpretations.

This view is reinforced by the fact that an advertisement for
the same television set appeared at about the same time in a
magazine called *Shuukan Asahi* (Weekly Asahi) (14 June 1985),
but this time with not a trace of sexual innuendo. This is a
'respectable' publication, roughly equivalent to the supplement
to *The Independent on Sunday* in Britain. The advertiser seems to
have chosen a completely different advertisement for *Shuukan
Asahi* because he thought that its readers were likely to find
sexually suggestive advertisements unacceptable. The illustration shows a middle-aged woman, apparently a housewife, a
schoolboy with a baseball cap, a young woman with a magazine, and a young boy, apparently a student. They are all
hanging onto straps of the type found in underground trains
and watching a miniature television set, except for the young
woman, who is looking at the camera. The caption reads:

51

(25) *Chikagoro, tsuukin-densha ga shumi desu.*
recently   commuting-train NOM hobby COP

Recently the commuting-train has become my hobby.

Because three of the characters are watching television, a further interpretation can be derived:

(26) Recently, watching television on commuter trains has become my hobby.

The contrast with the other two advertisements is strengthened by the fact that the English caption (21), common to both the earlier advertisements, has been replaced by the following Japanese caption:

(27) *Itsudemo   dokodemo   TV   taimu.*
whenever wherever TV time

TV-time, anytime, anywhere.

In (27), the only possible topic is 'television time', whereas in (21) the topic is not specified and it is not clear to what 'OK' might refer. From (27) interpretation (28) can thus safely be derived:

(28) You can watch television anywhere at any time.

The use of sexual imagery to promote products which are not obviously 'sexual' can be illustrated from the following British example (see Plate 3.3). This caption from *Elle* (British edition, December 1992) promotes Ellesse watches:

(29) Designed to perform.

This is accompanied, in smaller type, by:

(30) Ellesse watches, style with sports action.

A set of technical features are then detailed in a text in even smaller type, and an illustration shows a man and a woman who seem by their costume to be two swimmers. The audience would be encouraged to recover:

(31) Ellesse watches are designed to perform well in sporting situations in which a good watch is necessary.

But the illustration also has strong overtones of a relationship between the two figures. They are holding each other in a rather

Plate 3.3 Ellesse

intimate way, with the man's hand on the woman's thigh. The whole picture is in a provocative shade of red. The audience could thus also easily recover:

(32) Ellesse watches help you with sexual performance.

But the advertiser can easily deny that he ever meant to communicate (32).

Human susceptibility to certain phenomena may account for the easy recovery of sexual interpretations. The slightest hint of sex draws an audience's attention, because the cognitive system of human beings is organised in such a way that it is more susceptible to this kind of information than to other kinds. Generally, covert communication manipulates triggers to which the human mind is highly susceptible.

Covert communication can also appeal to what is only a slightly less 'basic' instinct in human beings, namely snobbery (Pearson and Turner 1966: 22–35; Packard 1961: 269–79). Advertisements for perfume are a particularly good example of this, for perfume is a luxury good, which is closely associated with wealth and status. Recent disputes over discounts on perfume offered at cut-price pharmaceutical chain stores in Britain show that the high price of perfumes is part of their prestige. The intrinsic worth of perfumes, in terms of costs of production, is greatly inflated by artificially induced scarcity and price manipulation. According to an advertiser working for a Japanese agency represented in London (personal communication), there is little demand for middle-range perfumes in Japan, so all imported brands of perfume are classified as top range. They are then priced at that level, regardless of their price in the country of origin, thus maintaining the luxury status of foreign perfume.

The following captions illustrate the appeal to notions of wealth and status:

(33) The costliest perfume in the world. (Joy, Jean Patou)
(34) Proudly announce a limited edition of our exclusive perfume. Available only at Harrods. (Sheherazade, Jean Desprez)

These captions may at first sight appear to be merely informative, but this is unlikely. Information that a perfume is the most expensive in the world, as in (33), could be counterproductive.

The most sensible audience reaction would be to say that one would never be so foolish as to buy such a costly brand if one could get another cheaper. This is clearly not the advertiser's aim. The underlying and covertly communicated message is:

(35) If you are someone who is extremely rich, you will want to display your wealth by buying this perfume.

The fact that a perfume manufacturer has an exclusive arrangement with Harrods, an upmarket department store in London, as in (34), carries similarly strong but covert implications about wealth and social status. However, an advertiser would want to avoid overtly communicating such a message as (35), because of its vulgar and disagreeably crude appeal.

Another aspect of perfume advertisements which appears to belong to the realm of covert communication concerns the abundant use of French for captions in perfume advertisements in both Japan and Britain. Small print in English and Japanese sometimes indicates where the perfume is available, but it is very discrete and many perfume advertisements carry captions in French alone.

The effect of such use of French is not properly linguistic, which 'begins when an utterance . . . is manifestly chosen by the speaker for its semantic properties' (Sperber and Wilson 1986a: 178). What is communicated by the use of the French language, such as assumptions about Frenchness, is not governed by grammar. It would be more accurate to say that this is an example of the effect of the property of stimuli. For example, there are various ways in which the message that I am Japanese can be communicated. I can say, 'I'm Japanese', in which case the message is conveyed by virtue of the semantic properties of my utterance. In this case, linguistic communication proper has occured. However, when I am speaking English my accent may also convey the message that I am Japanese, without my saying so. In this case, the message is conveyed by virtue of the property of the stimulus, and not via linguistic communication as such. Other examples of communication through the property of stimulus would include a sad intonation of voice in spoken communication, where the message that I am sad is communicated because of my sad sounding voice, and not because of my linguistic message.

The following captions provide such examples. (36) appeared

in a British magazine (see Plate 3.4), whereas (37) was found in a Japanese magazine:

(36) *Shiseido haute parfumerie des essences pures et identifiables.* (Feminité du Bois, Shiseido)

Shiseido, high quality perfume, made from essences which are pure and identifiable.

(37) *C'est la Vie! le parfum de Christian Lacroix.* (C'est la Vie, Christian Lacroix)

That's life! the perfume of Christian Lacroix.

One might imagine that the popularity of the French language in perfume advertisements is partly because the French have historically dominated perfume production, but it seems to relate more to a facet of snobbery. France is universally regarded as superior in matters relating to fashion, so that an understanding of things French in this domain is a sign of one's social standing. The advertiser flatters the addressee, a strategy which is alleged to be successful in advertising (Dyer 1982: 83). He employs captions which are relatively easy to translate, certainly for a British audience, but which could leave a warm glow of satisfaction in an addressee who has understood them. Thus every word in (36) corresponds fairly closely to an English word in both spelling and meaning, if one accepts that the phrase 'haute couture' has effectively become part of the English language. And 'C'est la vie!' in (37) is a widely used and understood catch-phrase in English-speaking countries.

Shiseido's advertising strategy throws interesting light on these points. It is a large Japanese cosmetics company, which has set up a wholly owned subsidiary in France to manufacture and market the perfume Feminité du Bois. When it moved into Western markets, it made Paris its headquarters and used French in its advertising campaigns. According to a public relations person from Shiseido London (personal communication), the perfume is available in Europe and North America, but not in Japan. The French caption in (36), according to her, is 'perfume-speak', and 'understandable to [Shiseido's] British audience'. It seems that Shiseido likes to benefit from French associations, without openly endorsing a claim to being a French company. This is one of the classic functions of covert communication.

Plate 3.4 Shiseido

CONCLUSION

In many cases, the advertiser intends to transmit some information and he intends to make his audience recognise that information, but he does not want to affect the mutual cognitive environment which he shares with his audience. At the most general level, this is because he wishes to draw attention away from the reason for his interacting with his audience. In more specific cases, he wishes to avoid the social implications that such a modification of the mutual cognitive environment might bring with it. In the examples discussed, sex and snobbery have been suggested as two areas of particular sensitivity to audience reactions (Tanaka 1990b, 1995).

Addressees are often helped to recover covertly communicated assumptions by various additional stimuli, which can act as an aid to the fulfilment of the communicator's informative intention. In a similar vein, Crompton (1987: 62) argues that effective headlines tell the audience one part of the story, while the picture tells the rest:

> Sometimes a headline can make no sense at all on its own. And a picture on its own can be a mystery. When the two come together, however, the whole story is revealed – with punch and originality.

Covert communication, if and when it works, allows the advertiser to 'have his cake and eat it'. When addressees recover assumptions about sex or status and respond positively, they may have a feeling of solidarity with the advertiser for being daring, interesting, or 'in the know'. The communicator seems merely to intend to 'trigger' certain concepts of sex or snobbery, and it is not crucial for him whether his audience believes his message to be true. Certainly, he cannot be held responsible if the product or service advertised does not enhance the love life or the social standing of people who purchase it. And he escapes responsibility for any negative social reactions emanating from the public.

4

PUNS

INTRODUCTION

In the previous chapter it was noted that the lack of trust and social co-operation between communicator and addressee creates problems for the advertiser, and it is suggested in this chapter that humour, more specifically punning, is one way in which the advertiser attempts to improve social relations with his audience. If the addressee thinks that the advertiser is witty and amusing, it may go some way to overcoming her distrust of him. As Crompton (1987: 39) puts it, one of the main advertising strategies is 'Make 'em laugh'.

Puns are usually assumed to have a low intellectual status, in spite of the fact that they are one of the most common forms of speech play. Redfern (1984: 4) cites Lionel Duisit, who describes puns as the 'least literary' of figures of speech, and Dryden, who calls them 'the lowest and most grovelling kind of wit'. Culler (1988: 4), for his part, quotes Pope's dismissal of the pun: 'he that would pun would pick a pocket'. Sherzer (1985: 215) argues that today puns are 'most often considered to be humorous in intention, inappropriate for serious discourse'. They are often used as 'the witty comebacks of conversation stoppers and the punch line of jokes'.

Redfern (1984: 130) suggests that advertisers share the literary critics' low opinion of puns and of humour in general. He wrote to twenty of the largest international advertising agencies to ask about the status of wordplay in advertising, and the most common response was that it was out of date to pun in advertisements. He also quotes Hopkins, an ex-advertiser: 'Frivolity has no place in advertising. Nor has humour. Spending money is

usually a serious business . . . People do not buy from clowns'
(Redfern 1984: 130).

The discrepancy between such views and the ubiquity of puns
and other forms of humour in British advertising may reflect
changing trends, which tend to swing rapidly back and forth in
the world of advertising (Cook 1992: 218–23). Redfern's research
was carried out prior to 1984 and the remark by Hopkins was
originally published as far back as 1927. Pearson and Turner
(1966: 64) refer to advertisers frowning on humour in advertising and deciding to give it up in the early 1960s. They echo
Hopkins, citing an advertiser's view that: 'Buying is a serious
business. Nobody buys from clowns'. And yet they note that in
reality 'humour provides one of the few discernible trade marks
of British advertising from the mid-nineteenth century'.

The mismatch between principles and practice is more con-
vincingly explained by Redfern on the grounds that the advertisers whom he contacted reflected the age-old embarrassment
connected with humour, and especially puns. They wished to
uphold the dignity of their profession. He points out that the
information supplied to him was flagrantly contradicted by
advertisements for the McDonald's hamburger chain, which
make liberal use of a clown figure. Advertisers are perhaps
unwilling to talk about their use of puns and other forms of
humour, attempting to dissociate themselves from the intention
to use word-play.

PUNS, AMBIGUITY AND RELEVANCE THEORY

According to Attridge (1988: 140–1), the function of language is
usually taken to be 'the clean transmission of a pre-existing, self-
sufficient, unequivocal meaning'. Puns thus raise the awkward
problem of 'the presence of ambiguity in language'. According
to *Collins English Language Dictionary* (1987: 1164), a pun can be
defined as 'a use of words that have more than one meaning, or
words that have the same sound but different meanings, so that
what you say has two different meanings and makes people
laugh'. When a word has several meanings, one speaks of
homonyms. When several words sound the same, they are called
homophones (Culler 1988: 4–5). Homophones and homonyms can
be whole phrases rather than single words, and similarities
between words and phrases do not have to be absolute to have

the ambiguous effect of a pun (Nash 1985: 137–47). As discussed in Chapter 2, it is necessary to distinguish unresolvable ambiguity from mere *underdeterminacy*, which is far more frequently encountered. The success of communication depends on the hearer's recovery of the speaker's intended interpretation, and not merely on her recognition of its linguistic meaning (Sperber and Wilson 1986a: 23). So communication can succeed when there is more than one possible interpretation of the utterance, as long as the speaker's intended interpretation is recoverable. Underdetermined utterances are so ubiquitous in ordinary communication that it is difficult to find any utterance which does not require some degree of disambiguation, reference assignment or enrichment. However, any such underdeterminacy is almost invariably resolved in context.

In contrast, there are cases in which the hearer is unable to identify the interpretation intended by the speaker, and such unrecoverable ambiguity is called *equivocation*. An utterance becomes *equivocal* when the hearer is unable to assign it a single intended interpretation. Such utterances are then interpreted as ambiguous, and the hearer has to seek clarification in order to recover the speaker's intention. Communication fails altogether when ambiguity is unresolvable, because the hearer cannot determine the speaker's intentions.

Attridge (1988: 141) says that the pun is not just ambiguous but that it is 'ambiguity *unashamed of itself*' (his italics). He points out that language works well in spite of its polysemous nature, because context acts as a disambiguating device. However, in the case of a pun:

> In place of a context designed to suppress latent ambiguity, the pun is the product of a context deliberately constructed to *enforce* an ambiguity, to render impossible the choice between meanings, to leave the reader or hearer endlessly oscillating in semantic space. (author's italics)

But there is an underlying assumption in his argument that a context is determined prior to an utterance, an assumption which in Chapter 2 has been shown to be false.

Leach (1976: 25) takes a different line from Attridge, stating that a pun 'forbids us to recognise that the sound pattern is ambiguous'. In this view, the audience does not recognise a pun's ambiguity because there is something about the pun which prevents such a recognition. Leach's comment is acceptable only insofar as the ambiguity of a pun is intentional and usually resolvable. The audience should be able to identify the intended interpretation of the speaker, which is the key to successful communication. However, it is incorrect to say that audiences do not simultaneously recognise the ambiguity of puns. On the contrary, the conscious recognition of multiple interpretations is essential for an audience to process an utterance as a pun. An audience appreciates the ambiguity of a pun as necessary for its success, and does not see ambiguity as a sign of failure in this kind of communication.

From the Relevance Theory point of view, a pun functions as follows: two or more interpretations are intentionally triggered by the speaker of a pun, but the hearer rejects the most accessible interpretations in search of a more acceptable interpretation. The speaker usually intends to communicate a single interpretation which the hearer has to recover, although, occasionally, more than one interpretation has to be combined to reach the ultimate message. It is manifest to both speaker and hearer that the speaker intends her to notice more than one interpretation. In most cases, only one interpretation is intended to be retained, and it is made mutually manifest that the other interpretations are to be rejected in favour of the one intended by the speaker. When a communicator intends two meanings to be recovered, they reinforce one another in some way. Thus the essence of the pun lies in its access to multiple interpretations. For a pun to be successful it is necessary that the addressee should access more than one interpretation of a given utterance. Ultimately, the speaker communicates a single message, even if he intends to activate two or more interpretations.

PUNS IN ADVERTISING

Puns are popular with advertisers in both Britain and Japan, whatever advertisers may say. It has been suggested that the British may be fonder of puns in advertising than any other nation in Europe. *The Independent* (1 July 1992) quotes Simon Anholt, of the multilingual copy-writing service Translators in Advertising: 'The British like humour, especially irony and puns. But you have to change this for the Germans and Swedes, who say that they don't buy from clowns'. There are also indications that the general public in Japan is fond of puns. An advertising campaign for a prestigious bookstore indicates that puns can even enjoy high intellectual status in Britain. The following examples have been selected from captions used in a campaign run by Dillons bookstore, after it was taken over by a multinational corporation:

(1) a We're literally about to open.
     b Literally the finest store in Europe.
     c Foiled again. Try Dillons.
     d Book now for Christmas.
     e High brows raised here.
     f Browsers Welcome. (High brows and low brows).
     g Over 5 miles of books.
        And they're all way over your head.
     h Materially supplied for seats of learning.
     i If you think this station's deep
        You should see our poetry department.
     j Go to Dillons. And be transported.

Most of these puns are fairly easy to resolve, although (1c) relies on knowledge that the main London competitor of Dillons is Foyles, which is not unknown for the poor organisation of its stock. Captions (1i) and (1j) rely for their effect on the fact that they were displayed in the London underground.

This campaign was seen as successful. According to their advertising agent (personal communication), Dillons regards itself as catering to the intellectual population not only of London, but also of Britain, and even possibly of Europe. It thought that punning would appeal to its target audience because of its wit and humour, and it was happy with the outcome of the campaign.

Puns are also a prominent form of wordplay in Japanese advertisements, and punning does not seem to be considered an inferior advertising strategy (Kitamura, Yamaji and Tabuki 1981: 91–103). According to Yamakawa and Nakamura (1985: 12) 'The forceful combination of two separate words creates a surprising world and widens the image of a product'. They give the following example from a television advertisement:

(2) *Kochira*   *minami-hankyuu,*   *kochira* *kita*
     this   south-hemisphere,   this   north

no Hankyuu.
of Hankyuu.

This is the southern hemisphere. This is Hankyuu
(Department Store) in the Northern District (of Osaka).

The word *hankyuu* can mean either 'hemisphere' or 'Hankyuu
Department Store', and the advertisement first shows a picture
of tropical islands in the South Pacific, and then a picture of a
department store in North Osaka.

Various attempts have been made to explain the prevalence of
punning in advertising, but none of them are satisfactory.
Sherzer (1985: 215) simply observes that puns are 'highly appropriate for advertising', without substantiating his claim.
According to Redfern:

> Advertising space is costly. Economy is essential, and
> puns are highly economical (two meanings for the price of
> one word or phrase), and are in fact much more of a
> labour-saving device than many of the products they seek
> to promote.
>
> (Redfern 1984: 130)

But advertisers do not usually intend their puns to communicate
two meanings. Moreover, the effort made by an audience in
recovering the intended effects of the advertisement is actually
increased by punning.

Relevance Theory provides the best framework for analysing
the role of puns in advertising, especially in regard to the
question of processing effort. Even though puns require greas-
ter processing effort than straightforward utterances, extra contextual effects are yielded which outweigh the greater effort. In
other words, puns achieve optimal relevance despite extra processing effort, because this is the most economical way to
achieve a full range of intended contextual effects. Wordplay in
advertising can thus be analysed in terms of the interpretation
process involved.

Advertisers deliberately cause their audience extra processing
effort by employing puns, because the first and perhaps the
most important requirement of an advertisement is that it
should attract and hold an audience's attention (Dyer 1982: 139).
As Cook (1992: 217) says:

Another reason for this impression of restlessness is that ads, for many people, are either not at the centre of attention or do not hold attention for long. Ads come in short bursts. While they may momentarily amuse or attract, their nature changes under scrutiny. Their brief is to gain and hold attention, fix a name with positive associations, and go. Yet many ads do not succeed in attracting attention at all . . . They are uninvited, embedded in another discourse such as a TV programme, newspaper article or mail delivery, which, for the recipient, is more important. For these reasons, ads often exist on the periphery of receiver attention.

Extra processing effort may therefore be said to be the price which the advertiser has to pay to get his message noticed at all. Without an 'attention-grabbing' device such as a pun, an audience might pay no attention to an advertisement, which would thus achieve no effects at all. Moreover, solving a pun can help to retain attention, so that an opinion which the addressee might scarcely notice is strengthened because of the extra processing effort involved.

The taxonomy of puns is not a concern of this chapter, in that the assignment of an utterance to a particular type of pun is not part of what is communicated and does not play a necessary role in comprehension. However, puns will be considered here under four headings. There are puns whose initial meaning is nonsensical and has to be rejected in favour of another interpretation, which is the one intended by the communicator. In some cases, the rejected interpretations nevertheless help in some way to obtain additional contextual effects which are intended by the speaker. In yet other cases, the advertiser takes advantage of a pun to communicate a message which he would otherwise not be able to communicate without risking a claim of indecency. Lastly, there are puns which come close to Redfern's notion of 'two meanings for the price of one', in that more than one interpretation is intended by the communicator. However, the boundaries between these types of pun are far from clearcut, and are rather a matter of degree. All four kinds of puns can be found in advertising.

'NONSENSE' PUNS

An advertisement for London Transport, which appeared in London tube stations and trains in 1981, had the following caption:

(3) Less bread. No jam.

Reading the words 'bread' and 'jam', the addressee will probably take the words to mean foodstuffs. These would be the most accessible interpretations, as bread and jam are stereotypical items of consumption in Britain, whether separately or together. But such interpretations will have to be rejected as inconsistent with the principle of relevance, for the caption advertises London Transport. Having put aside the first interpretation to come to mind, the addressee would hopefully remember that 'bread' is slang for 'money', while 'jam' can also mean 'traffic jam'. She would then recover the following propositional form:

(4) Less money, no traffic jam.

She would then have to resolve some further indeterminacies, such as what it is that costs less money and for whom. Since the advertisement is promoting London Transport, something like the following should be recovered:

(5) If you travel by London Transport, it will cost you less than travelling by car, and you will not suffer in traffic jams.

Although this may seem ironical when the audience reads it, jammed into a rush-hour train, it is unlikely that it was intended by the advertiser to be so.

The pun activates two sets of interpretations, but ultimately communicates a single set of interpretations. The only set of interpretations which the advertiser intends his audience to retain is 'bread' as 'money' and 'jam' as 'traffic jam'. The 'food' interpretations are intended to be accessed first, but then rejected. The advertiser does not endorse them, for they are irrelevant to the service promoted by the advertisement. That is why the audience will continue to search for another interpretation. Redfern's claim that the pun provides 'two meanings for the price of one word or phrase' is clearly not borne out in this case.

Nor can it be said that the caption fits Redfern's notion of the pun as a 'labour-saving device', in that the addressee has to expend considerable extra processing effort in order to recover the intended ultimate meaning. The advertiser could easily have used the words 'money' and 'traffic jam', so he must have been aware that these interpretations would probably not be the first ones to be recovered by his addressee from the words which he actually employed. The addressee has to reject the first accessible meanings of 'bread' and 'jam', and search in her memory for more acceptable interpretations. Moreover, 'money' may not be a highly accessible interpretation of the word 'bread' in Britain, for it is American slang in origin.

The following is a Japanese example of a pun which belongs to this category. It is a caption of an advertisement for toothbrushes (Lion, found in *Asahi Advertising Prize 1983/1984*: 29; see Plate 4.1). The accompanying illustration shows an open-mouthed crocodile, whose jaws consist of two toothbrushes:

(6) *Hito   wa   ha-chuui-rui*
    human   TOP   tooth-attention-species

However there is not such a word as *ha-chuui-rui* in Japanese. It is similar to another word *hachuurrui* meaning 'reptile'. Partly because of this similarity in sound, and partly because of the illustration, (6) would activate (7):

(7) Humans are reptiles.

However, (7) is clearly false, as humans are not reptiles. Moreover (7) is irrelevant to the fact that it is a caption for a toothbrush advertisement. The word *ha-chuui-rui* is written in three Chinese characters, meaning 'tooth-attention-species'. The audience would thus reject the first accessible interpretation and recover (8) and then (9):

(8) Humans are a tooth-attention-species.
(9) Humans are a species which pays attention to teeth.

The pun in (6) activates the interpretation (7) which is then rejected, because it is nonsense and irrelevant, for (9), the interpretation the advertiser intended to communicate.

Another example in this category comes from a poster in a British railway station:

(10) Mind your own business. Move it to Milton Keynes.

The expression 'mind your own business' usually means:

(11) Do not concern yourself with other people's affairs.

But this does not yield enough relevance to outweigh the addressee's processing effort, as she would have no idea to whose affairs it refers. She would then search for alternative interpretations, and would hopefully remember that 'mind' can mean 'look after' and that 'business' can mean 'firm' or 'company'. The second part of the caption should also suggest this interpretation, especially as the addressee knows that it is an advertisement, because of its location. Additional text written below provides further clues:

(12) Curious to find out why so many top British companies are moving to Milton Keynes?

The addressee should then derive (13) from the first part of (10):

(13) Look after your own company.

Together with the latter part of the caption, further contextual effects should arise, such as (14):

(14) You can improve your company's prospects by moving it to Milton Keynes.

Puns attract attention because they frustrate initial expectations of relevance and create a sense of surprise. They arouse an addressee's interest by making her think, 'What on earth does that mean?' The purpose is not to convey a novel idea, for there are few new things to say about many products. As Crompton (1987: 36) puts it: 'When you have nothing to say, use showmanship'. Creating a puzzle is one way of trying to make a stale message more appealing.

It is especially important for advertisers to divert an audience's attention away from a message which is either expected or boring (Crompton 1987: 172–4). Thus the captions noted above would almost certainly be more successful in attracting attention than captions such as (15) to (17):

(15) Take the tube: it is cheaper and more convenient.
(16) Brush your teeth with a Lion toothbrush.
(17) Milton Keynes is a good location for businesses.

Some captions may also succeed in attracting attention because they seem negative, whereas advertisements are expected to promise an abundance of good things. Thus Cook (1992: 222) says: 'If an ad departs from expectation it will attract attention'. The London Transport caption seems to promise to reduce the supply of desirable foodstuffs. Jam often has an especially strong meaning of something pleasant or desirable, as in the expression 'jam tomorrow'. The toothbrush advertisement's description of humans as reptiles is not exactly a compliment to its audience. The Milton Keynes advertisement seems to treat its audience as though they had been nosy. Advertisements are expected to say nice things to the audience, and not to call them names or to rebuke harshly. These captions strike their audiences by talking about desirable things in a negative way, setting up a challenge which the audience is tacitly invited to solve.

Another example of a 'negative' advertisement is that for the National Army Museum, which appeared in the London underground system:

(18)   If you think your journey's hell, try catching the 1815
       to Waterloo.

The first interpretation of this might be that the advertiser is offering long-suffering commuters an even worse train journey. But as a commuter train would be unlikely to be going into Waterloo at quarter past six in the evening, the addressee should recover the interpretation of 1815 as a date and of Waterloo as the battle and not the railway station. This second interpretation is reinforced by a picture of the battle of Waterloo and (19) in small print:

(19)   Come and see the world's largest reconstruction of the
       most famous battle in history at the Road to Waterloo
       Gallery.

The advertiser has in effect attracted his audience's attention by initially appearing to offer them something even worse than their present plight.

Once attention has been attracted, the advertiser's main desire is that his audience should consider, like, and remember the advertisement (Dyer 1982: 139–40). Because a pun takes longer to process, it sustains the addressee's attention over a

Plate 4.1 Lion

period of time, and, once comprehended, it is often remembered. Some people do not recover a pun's message immediately and think about it until they finally see the light. They may ask someone else what it could possibly mean, thereby spreading information about the advertisement. Solving a pun can give rise to a pleasant feeling, springing from a kind of intellectual satisfaction. The addressee congratulates herself and may think of the product in congenial terms as a result. She may also tell others about an advertisement which she thinks is clever or unusual. Even if some people find a pun obscure or irritating, this will still be welcomed by the advertiser, for he considers that in terms of product recognition any reaction is better than none. Increased memorability is thus a major advantage derived from more processing effort.

The humorous side to puns may be especially important in achieving the advertiser's goals in certain social situations. A large number of advertisements using puns have been found in locations related to public transport, where the advertiser has a captive and bored audience, who appreciate a little entertainment to relieve their misery. By offering an amusing pun, the advertiser provides his audience with the desired entertainment, and thus makes them feel congenial towards the product which he is promoting. He simultaneously overcomes some of the distrust which the audience feels towards him.

In short, the use of the pun ensures that the message is communicated with more 'strength' than might otherwise have been possible, a necessity in advertising. An advertiser is particularly concerned with the problem of attracting and holding an audience's attention, for there is a particularly high initial probability of an audience taking no notice at all of the communicator's message. The ostensive stimulus which an advertiser uses thus remains the most economical means which he needs to employ in order to achieve his intended effects.

In the examples above, the interpretation which the advertiser intends to be rejected is irrelevant to the interpretation he intends eventually to communicate, but this does not mean that the rejected interpretation is chosen entirely at random. It may give rise to some effects in its own right. The London Transport advertisement reads initially as if it were about food, a topic 'loaded with hidden meanings' (Packard 1981: 87). Indeed, food words are often used in Britain to promote technology, as in the

'Apple', 'Apricot' and 'Peach' brand names for computers and software. In the National Army Museum example, the advertiser may be appealing to a British tradition of keeping a stiff upper lip in unpleasant circumstances.

PUNS AND CONTEXT

In another kind of pun, rejected interpretations actually contribute to the intended interpretation. The rejected interpretation provides access to encyclopaedic information, which is then used in processing the intended interpretation. This contributes additional contextual effects to the interpretation which the advertiser ultimately intends to communicate to his audience.

An excellent example of this type of pun is provided by the caption for a 1977 Guinness advertisement in Britain, found in Redfern (1984: 134). It appeared in the year of the Queen's Silver Jubilee:

(20) We've poured throughout her reign.

The addressee begins by disambiguating the word 'pour', which can mean either 'flow' or 'serve liquid'. As it is an advertisement for beer, she is most likely to select the 'serve liquid' interpretation. Then she must assign reference to the pronoun 'we'. From her experience, she would know that the word 'we' in advertisements could refer to the advertiser, the audience, characters in the advertisement, or the firm making the product advertised. Because of the verb 'pour' which follows, she will probably assume that 'we' means the Guinness company, as it provides beer. The pronoun 'her' will be more easily assigned to mean 'the Queen's', because it is followed by the word 'reign', and the advertisement is appearing in the Queen's Silver Jubilee year. The following proposition will then be recovered:

(21) The Guinness company has served beer for as long as the Queen has been on the throne.

However, the addressee is unlikely to stop there, because the advertiser has deliberately omitted the word 'beer' after the verb. The caption could just as easily have read:

(22) We've poured beer throughout her reign.

The addition of the word 'beer' would have substantially inhibited any further interpreting of the caption, whereas the truncated form of the proposition expressed encourages further processing.

The addressee is thus likely to think of 'pour' in the sense of 'pour down' or 'fall', and to interpret 'reign' as 'rain'. There are two homophones of 'reign', but 'rain' is the most accessible one. The prior occurrence of the word 'pour' will encourage the addressee to think of 'rain' rather than 'rein'. The image of 'pouring rain' will be within easy reach because of the kind of weather to which people living in Britain are accustomed. And once 'pouring rain' is activated, it will give the addressee access to her encyclopaedic knowledge, which may include the fact that rainy weather is associated with the Queen, for it is commonly believed that it tends to rain on royal occasions. Thus the caption sets out to activate two sets of meanings, even if it only explicitly communicates one through the use of the spelling 'reign'.

The advantage to the advertiser of the pun is that the association between 'beer' and 'rain' can yield information to be added to the context in which the advertisement is finally processed, as extra implicated assumptions. Guinness has traditionally presented an image of its product as a 'national drink', and this image is subtly reinforced by the pun associating beer with rain. The advertisement came out in the unusually wet summer of 1977, when 'pouring rain' would more than ever appear as a typical national phenomenon. Joking about the weather is a prominent British characteristic, which is alluded to by the use of the pun. Each of these additional contextual effects serves to enhance the desired image of Guinness as an integral part of Britain's national heritage, even though it can be argued that Guinness is in reality an Irish beer. Moreover, Guinness has an old and well established reputation for humorous advertising, which it may have wanted to restore after a period of turning away from it in the 1960s (Pearson and Turner 1966: 64–75).

The next example is a caption for All Nipon Airways, promoting its Hawaii flight:

(23) *Ha ha ha wai wai wai.*

The transcription is all in *katakana*, the marked form of Japanese syllabic script, which is used for things such as onomatopoeias,

Western loan words, and exclamations, as opposed to the unmarked *hiragana*. *Ha ha ha* and *wai wai wai* are both onomatopoeias, and the former, just as in English, indicates a laughing noise and the latter a lively noise made by a crowd. Thus, (23) would seem to express noises made by a large and happy crowd.

However, these interpretations will be rejected by the audience, as inconsistent with the fact that it is an advertisement for an airline company. Having rejected the first interpretation to come to mind, and aided by the fact that it is an airline company and that *katakana* can be used for Western words, the audience will recover (24):

(24) Hawaii.

Although the audience of (23) have to thus reject the first accessible interpretation for the intended interpretation, the rejected interpretation gives rise to some effects. It triggers the recovery of some encyclopaedic knowledge about a large number of happy and noisy people. Hawaii is a holiday resort, which people visit to enjoy the sun, the beach and themselves. The association between a cheerful crowd and Hawaii may be added to the context in which the caption is finally processed, resulting in (25):

(25) In Hawaii a lot of people are enjoying themselves.

Thus, (23) triggers the interpretation to do with cheerful noises, which is rejected for the intended interpretation (24). However, when (24) is processed against the context containing the cheerful noises, (24) yields extra intended contextual effects such as (25).

Other examples of this type of pun appeared in a promenade concert programme on 10 September 1992:

(26) a Enjoy a great reception. (Cellnet) (see Figure 4.2)
    b We're in tune with your energy needs. (Powergen)
    c Always in the right key. (Budget)
    d The 'Opening Movement'. (Coca-Cola)
    e If you don't fit a Blaupunkt in your car
       how many notes will you really save? (Bosch Telecom)

The advertisers are trying to add special appeal for music lovers

Enjoy a great reception

We tune and retune our network to ensure every call is music to your ears. For more information please call 0800 214000. cellnet

Plate 4.2 Cellnet

attending the 'proms'. In each example, the first interpretation to be activated has to do with music and will need to be rejected for the intended interpretation to be eventually recovered. However, the additional contextual assumptions about music give rise to intended contextual effects. The advertisers hope that a music-loving audience will feel congenial towards these contextual effects, and that such feelings will be transferred to the product which is being advertised.

PUNS AND SEXUAL INNUENDO

A pun may be used by an advertiser who wants to communicate something, but does not wish to do so overtly, and it thus shares aspects of covert communication, as discussed in the previous chapter. This can be a particularly useful device when an advertiser wishes to insinuate things which are too indecent for him to say outright. Another All Nippon Airways advertisement promoting a flight to Okinawa (see Plate 4.3), an island in the far south of Japan, falls into this category:

(27)   *Oo Kli NAa <u>WAh</u>.*

The capital letters correspond to larger characters in the Japanese original. The underlined letters are in *katakana* and the rest is in *hiragana*.

By picking up the larger letters only, it reads 'o-ki-na-wa', that is, 'Okinawa', the destination of the promoted flight. Reading all the letters, it reads 'oo-kii-naa-wah', where *ookii* means 'big', *naa* is an exclamation particle, and *wah is* an exclamation like 'wow'. Thus, there are two possible readings of this caption:

(28)   Okinawa.
(29)   How big! Wow!

Interpretation (29) raises the question as to what it is which is *ookii* (big). There are at least two possible candidates: Okinawa Island, which is the destination of the flight promoted in the advertisement, and the big breasts of the girl shown in the illustration. These interpretations would lead to either (30) or (31):

(30)   In Okinawa, there is lots of space.
(31)   In Okinawa, there are a lot of beautiful girls with big breasts.

This example may be regarded as a case of deliberate equivocation, or unresolvable ambiguity. There is an element of covertness here, for the advertiser does not intend to convey (31) on the basis of making his intention to inform (31) mutually manifest. The pun may be chiefly an attention-getting device, with the 'space' interpretation being the only one ostensively communicated. Additional contextual effects about the sort of desirable girls holiday-makers will find in Okinawa are more or less covertly communicated.

All Nippon Airways seems to think that space is an important attraction for their audience. They used the following caption for their flight to Hokkaidoo, Japan's northern island:

(32)   *Dekkai-doo Hokkaidoo.*
       huge-EMPH Hokkaidoo

Plate 4.3 All Nippon Airways

which could be interpreted as (33):

(33) It is huge, Hokkaidoo.

Dekkai, the colloquial word for 'big', and the emphatic *doo* are used for their phonetic similarities to the phrase name *Hokkaidoo*.

The following caption for Four Corners honeymoon holidays is similar to the Okinawa example in that the pun allows the advertiser to say something he would otherwise be unable to say:

(34) After you get married, kiss your wife in places she's never been kissed before.

The advertisement shows different illustrations of exotic honeymoon destinations. The word 'places' activates interpretation (35), which will then be rejected for interpretation (36) which the advertiser intends to communicate:

(35) After you get married, kiss your wife on parts of her body where she's never been kissed before.
(36) After you get married go on honeymoon and kiss your wife in locations in which she's never been kissed before.

In this case, unlike the Okinawa example, (35) is accessed as part of comprehension process of overt communication. Even though (35) is to be eventually rejected for (36), without the use of pun the advertiser might seem too indecent. The pun here turns an otherwise vulgar statement into humour. Leach (1976: 18) notes: 'Punning . . . is an extremely important feature of all forms of symbolic communication but especially perhaps in areas of social life which are the focus of taboo such as sex and religion.'

PUNS WITH TWO COMMUNICATED MEANINGS

Some puns do not just communicate one interpretation while activating another, but actually communicate both meanings. Redfern's comment that puns provide 'two meanings for the price of one word or phrase' is thus valid in these particular cases. The following caption for a Mazda car, which appeared at a train station in 1986, serves as an example:

(37) The perfect car for a long drive.

The advertisement shows a Mazda parked on a lengthy drive, which leads to a mansion. The word 'drive' can mean 'a car ride', and on this interpretation the audience would derive (38):

(38) The perfect car for a long ride.

This interpretation would yield a number of contextual effects, which include (39) and (40):

(39) The car is perfect for people who have to go on long car rides.

(40) The car functions well on a long ride.

However, 'drive' can also mean 'driveway' and the picture of a long driveway might encourage an alternative interpretation:

(41) The perfect car for people who have a long driveway.

The illustration also shows a large mansion to which the driveway leads, and this would encourage the addressee to extend her search for assumptions about life style. She might well derive further contextual effects, such as (42) and (43):

(42) The car is perfect for people who have a long driveway and a large mansion.

(43) The car is perfect for people who enjoy a comfortable life style.

Thus, the caption communicates both interpretations (38) and (41). They both yield substantial contextual effects, and it is not clear to the addressee which interpretation is intended by the communicator. There is no good reason to reject either interpretation as irrelevant, but they both seem insufficient or incomplete on their own.

In this case, the two interpretations together yield adequate contextual effects for no unjustifiable processing effort, and are thus consistent with the principle of relevance. The communicator intends his addressee to process and retain both interpretations, together with their effects. Furthermore, despite the independence of the two interpretations, they can combine with the additional premise, as in (44):

(44) People who have a long driveway are the sort of people who drive long distances.

The possibility that a pun may genuinely communicate 'two meanings for the price of one' would arise where neither of the two interpretations is sufficient on its own, but where the two jointly yield adequate effects for no unjustifiable effort in a way the advertiser could manifestly have foreseen.

A caption for women's underwear illustrates the same type of pun in which both meanings are intended to be communicated:

(45) Next to myself, I like Vedonis.

Vedonis is a brand name, and 'next to' can be interpreted either physically or more abstractly. If the addressee takes the more abstract interpretation, she will recover:

(46) After myself, I like Vedonis underwear.

But the addressee would think that it is strange to say this about underwear, for it is more common to say such a thing about one's mother, husband or child. Considering that it is an advertisement for underwear, which one wears next to one's skin, the addressee would find a physical interpretation also possible, and thus recover:

(47) On my skin, I like wearing Vedonis underwear.

This would give rise to further contextual effects, such as (48):

(48) Vedonis underwear feels good on one's skin.

The utterance used in this advertisement at first sight seems to be inconsistent with the principle of relevance, since the intended effects could have been more economically achieved. The communicator has again deliberately chosen an utterance which causes his addressee extra processing effort, when he could simply have made his character say:

(49) I like the feel of Vedonis on my skin.

However, the advertiser gains certain advantages from the extra processing effort imposed on his addressee, in addition to the ever present 'attention-catching' function of puns. Underwear is not meant to receive public exposure. Unlike other outfits chosen to appeal to a wide range of spectators, underwear is mainly chosen for functional reasons, such as the feel on the skin and the warmth it gives, or because it appeals to the wearer. Having recovered interpretation (46), to the effect that

Vedonis underwear is a favourite object, the addressee may conclude that the advertiser would like her to choose Vedonis on the grounds that she likes it, rather than because it is functional. The advertiser flatters the addressee's narcissism, overcoming the obstacle that she cannot show off the underwear to people outside a very close circle.

Taking this argument a step further, the brand name 'Vedonis' can be conceived of as a blend of the mythological figures 'Venus' and 'Adonis'. In Greek mythology, Adonis was loved by Aphrodite for his beauty, while Aphrodite was the goddess of love, corresponding to Roman Venus. Hence a further interpretation might arise:

(50) I like Venus and Adonis for their beauty, after myself.

This could in turn provide access to implicated assumptions, such as:

(51) Vedonis underwear is so beautiful that some people might like it best after themselves.

Such assumptions could be combined with the more physical interpretation (47) to implicate the following conclusion:

(52) I like Vedonis not only for its function, but also for its exceptional beauty.

Alternatively, the advertiser may have exploited the suggestion of a combination of Venus and Adonis further to tickle the audience's narcissism by suggesting (53):

(53) I like Venus and Adonis for their beauty, but only after myself.

When this hypothesis was tested on native English speakers, the only person to think of Venus and Adonis was an anthropologist, whose research interests included the language of advertising. It is possible that we both put more than the usual processing effort into interpretation, extending the search in our encyclopaedic memory to a greater degree than would a general audience. The advertiser could scarcely have expected all his addressees to be familiar with Greek and Roman mythology or to have such a high level of attention. But the advertiser may have hoped that the mythological resonances would be picked up by at least a few people in his audience.

In short, the advertiser could not have been more economical in achieving his intended effects, even though he makes his audience go through both abstract and physical interpretations of the caption. If he had chosen a straightforward utterance such as (48) or (49), the addressee would have missed additional implications to do with the exceptional beauty of the underwear. In deriving the interpretation intended by the communicator, the addressee is encouraged to process both abstract and physical interpretations. Then she will be given access to contextual assumptions which include the functional qualities of underwear, narcissism and mythological references. Thus, the relevance of (45) is established by recovering a wide range of weak contextual effects, arising from two distinct interpretations.

CONCLUSION

A pun is essentially a device to attract and retain an addressee's attention. For advertisers, more than for almost any other kind of communicator, it is crucial to attract the attention of audiences, and the pun is one of the linguistic devices most frequently exploited to this end. The extra processing effort needed to solve the pun helps to sustain the audience's attention for longer and makes the advertisement more memorable.

The audience gains extra contextual effects based on the pleasure and satisfaction of having solved the pun. These effects may affect the audience's attitude to the advertisement, and ultimately, the product advertised (Tanaka 1992).

The form which this processing effort takes varies according to the type of pun. Sometimes, additional interpretations are simply rejected, but in other cases they provide access to encyclopaedic information which is used in processing the intended interpretation, and thus give rise to additional contextual effects. Whatever the kind of pun, it is still the most economical way to achieve the full range of intended contextual effects.

This chapter not only explains how what appears to be a counter-example to Relevance Theory is usefully explained by the theory, but also makes a contribution to the wider debate on ambiguity. The pun is a case of intended ambiguity, involving two or more interpretations.

5

METAPHORS

INTRODUCTION

Tropes or figures of speech, that is words or expressions used in a figurative sense, are widely employed in advertising. This chapter concentrates on metaphor, examples of which abound in both British and Japanese advertising. Amongst tropes, metaphor is generally 'thought of as the fundamental "figure" of speech' (Hawkes 1984: 2). Much work could be done within a Relevance framework on other tropes encountered in advertising, such as irony, hyperbole, meiosis, simile, metonymy, and synecdoche, but this chapter confines itself to metaphor.

As Ortony (1979: 5) has observed, there is little agreement as to what constitutes metaphors and types of metaphor. Davidson (1979) states that metaphors cause the audience to see things in a new light, but that to see something in a new light is the work of imagination. This leaves the explanation as vague as the metaphors for which he is trying to account. According to the *Collins English Language Dictionary* (1987: 910), a metaphor is 'an imaginative way of describing something, by referring to something else which has the qualities that you are trying to express'. Thus a shy and timid person might be called a mouse. But this particular metaphor is highly 'standardised' (Sperber and Wilson 1986a: 236), that is, so commonly used that it is questionable whether it is an 'imaginative' description of such a person. At the other end of the scale are 'creative metaphors' (Sperber and Wilson 1986a: 236), which propose an unusual or unexpected correspondence between words or expressions.

Metaphors have usually been taken to be a form of non-literal utterance, but the psychological reality of the distinction between literal and non-literal utterances has been questioned by Rumelhart (1979). He argues that in language acquisition the comprehension process of metaphor is essentially the same as that of literal utterances. This suggests that literal and non-literal language use may involve the same comprehension process.

LAKOFF AND JOHNSON'S APPROACH TO METAPHOR

Lakoff and Johnson (1980: 3) follow the same line in their claim that the human thinking process is 'fundamentally metaphorical in nature'. They argue against the assumption that metaphors are a deviation from some arbitrarily defined 'normal' speech. Metaphor for them is not only 'a matter of . . . ordinary language', but also 'a matter of . . . thought and action'.

They distinguish between three kinds of metaphor (Lakoff and Johnson 1980: 14, 25). 'Structural metaphors' occur when one concept is 'metaphorically structured' on the basis of another. When a metaphorical concept 'organises', rather than 'structures' a whole system of concepts, they refer to it as an 'orientational metaphor'. 'Ontological metaphors' occur when human experience of physical objects and substances provides a basis for understanding abstract things, such as activities, emotions and ideas, of which we tend not to have direct knowledge. This allows us to relate more directly to them.

The underlying assumption behind Lakoff and Johnson's thinking is that the language we use in everyday life, including metaphor, is evidence of how we understand and experience things. They claim (1980: 4) that our ordinary conceptual system is fundamentally metaphorical, and that it is metaphors which structure our way of perceiving, thinking and acting. This type of framework or 'conceptual system' depends on the way we interact with our physical and cultural environments. Some of these conceptual systems will be universal, while others will be dependent on language and culture.

Lakoff and Johnson give examples of what they claim to be a pervasive English ontological metaphor: ARGUMENT IS WAR:

(1) Your claims are *indefensible*.
He *attacked every weak point* in my argument.
His criticisms were *right on target*.

I *demolished* his argument.

I've never *won* an argument with him.

(Lakoff and Johnson 1980: 4)

This conceptual system is not exclusive to the English language, for it carries over into Japanese:

(2) a *Kare   to   ii-araso-tta.*
    he   with   say-fight-PAST

   I argued with him.

  b *Kare   o   ii-makasi-ta.*
    he   ACC   say-beat-PAST

   I beat him in the argument.

  c *Futa-ri   wa   hageshiku   giron   o*
    two people TOP severely   discussion ACC

   tatakawa-se-ta.
   fight-CAUS-PAST

   The two had a severe discussion.

It seems reasonable to suggest that our perception and thinking processes are affected by the language we use, but Lakoff and Johnson claim more than this:

The metaphor [of war] is not merely in the words we use –
it is in our very concept of an argument. The language of
argument is not poetic, fanciful, or rhetorical; it is literal.

(Lakoff and Johnson 1980: 5)

Unfortunately, they do not define what they mean by 'literal'. However, it is clear that Lakoff and Johnson are referring to metaphor not just as a linguistic device, but also as a cognitive object. To say that there is some interaction between the metaphors we use in the particular natural language and the concepts we employ in perceiving and thinking is one thing; to say that they are identical is another, which is far harder to accept. The claim that the linguistic representation in a specific language is identical to the cognitive representation employed by the people of that linguistic community requires further evidence.

GRICE'S APPROACH TO METAPHOR

There has been a considerable amount of work in linguistics over the last two decades which claims that metaphors are best analysed in the domain of pragmatics (Grice 1975; Sperber and Wilson 1986a, 1995; Wilson and Sperber 1988b; Levinson 1983; Blakemore 1987, 1992; Wilson 1990). John Wilson (1990: 112) presents a consensus view among Gricean pragmatists that beneath the surface form of metaphors there is meaning, which is accessed through some model of conversational interaction. These pragmatists share the assumption that there is either one or more underlying principles which govern communication, and hence the understanding of metaphors.

Grice sees metaphor as violating his maxim of truthfulness: 'Do not say what you believe to be false.' A speaker who says that p indicates that he believes that p, that is to say that the proposition expressed by the speaker's utterance must be identical to a belief of the speaker. In such a framework, a metaphor has to be treated as a deviation from the norm, because the proposition expressed by the utterance containing a metaphor is not identical to the belief of the speaker. Hence, metaphors involve a deliberate violation of the maxim of truthfulness, and the comprehension of metaphorical utterances depends on the hearer finding the utterances to be false.

Grice gives as an example (3), which can be interpreted as a metaphor as in (4):

(3) You are the cream in my coffee.
(4) You are my pride and joy.

Let us see how Grice's schema looks in this example of metaphor. The schema is treated in an expanded form, in order to make it more workable:

(5) a He has said that I am the cream in his coffee.
 a′ This is obviously false.
 b There is no reason to suppose that he is not observing the truthfulness maxim at some level, though he is blatantly not doing so at the level of what he said.
 c He could not be doing this unless he thought that I have some of the features associated with cream in coffee.

c′ A likely feature is that of giving pleasure, adding something extra.

d He knows (and knows that I know that he knows) that I can see that the supposition that he thinks that I am his pride and joy is required.

e He has done nothing to stop me thinking that I am his pride and joy.

f He intends me to think, or at least is willing to allow me to think, that I am his pride and joy.

g And so, he has implicated that I am his pride and joy.

As discussed in Chapter 2, the content of the implicature which is introduced in (5c) is not deducible from either (5a) or (5b). Nowhere in this calculation is it explained how the hearer is expected to derive this particular implicature.

Grice's calculation becomes yet more problematic when he returns to this example (1975: 53), saying that it is possible 'to combine metaphor and irony' in a single utterance 'by imposing on the hearer two stages of interpretation'. According to this suggestion, the speaker, by uttering (3), intends the hearer to derive (4), and then go on to recover:

(6) You are my bane.

But Grice does not explain where the expression (6) comes from or how the hearer might derive (4) alone in some circumstances, rather than both (4) and (6).

Moreover, (4) is inherently a poor paraphrase of what the speaker intended to convey with (3). For example, the speaker may have intended to communicate something about the voluptuousness of the hearer with the metaphor of cream, which he cannot communicate with (4). Grice thus fails to account for the richness of metaphor, which is one of its advantages.

The following example of creative metaphor used by Sperber and Wilson (1986a: 237) illustrates this problem. It is Flaubert's comment on the poet Leconte de Lisle:

(7) *Son encre est pale.*
His ink is pale.

There is no paraphrasing (7) without losing its effects. In understanding the metaphor in (7), the hearer is urged to extend the context and look for a wide range of weakly communicated implications, such as that Leconte de Lisle's writing lacks contrasts, that it may fade and not survive over time, that his writing style is weak and characterless, and so on.

A RELEVANCE-BASED APPROACH TO METAPHOR

Wilson and Sperber (1988b: 139) deny the requirement for any maxim of truthfulness, and argue that there is no discontinuity between metaphorical and non-metaphorical utterances. They say that 'every utterance comes with a guarantee of faithfulness, not of truth'. In their view, every utterance is a faithful representation of a thought, but it is not necessarily identical with that thought. Thus a metaphorical utterance faithfully resembles a thought which the speaker intends to communicate.

Sperber and Wilson (1986a: 264) explain the indeterminacy and the richness of metaphor by treating it as a variety of 'loose talk', as discussed in Chapter 2. They treat metaphorical utterances as reflecting a different degree in the scale of 'resemblance' between the utterance used and the thought communicated. This applies to all cases of utterance interpretation, thus allowing them to account for metaphors and other less than literal utterances without abandoning truth-conditional semantics.

The notion of interpretive resemblance is crucial to their account. There is interpretive resemblance between a given utterance and the thought expressed by that utterance, if they resemble each other in sharing part of each other's content. Literalness is merely an extreme case in the scale of resemblance. Metaphors are the result of choosing an utterance which is a less than literal interpretation of the speaker's thought. The proposition expressed by the utterance shares some of the analytic and contextual implications of the thought which it resembles.

There is no clear definition as to which contextual effects are shared between metaphors and the thoughts which they resemble, because metaphors often convey an indeterminate range of thoughts. That is, the speaker intends to communicate a range of implicatures, rather than a fixed set. Communication succeeds when the hearer has recovered some of the implicatures within the range. The relevance of a metaphor to the hearer is established by recovering an array of implicatures.

Bencherif (unpublished) points out that the hearer, in her

search for optimal relevance, is forced to see a resemblance between the object featured in the metaphor and the object to which the metaphorical utterance refers. This may explain one of the advantages offered by metaphor. That is, the metaphor makes the hearer see some resemblance between things where she may not have seen it before.

The range and strength of recovered implicatures give rise to two broad types of metaphor. In the case of standardised metaphors, the addressee is encouraged to recover a narrow range of strong implicatures. In the case of creative metaphors, the addressee is forced to look for a wide range of weak implicatures.

The notion of weak communication, as discussed in Chapter 2, is important for the indeterminate nature of metaphors and the way in which they are processed by the hearer. The hearer's comprehension of an utterance, that is the assumptions which she infers from it, may not be limited to those which the speaker specifically intended her to recover. She may recover some implications which she infers on her own responsibility.

There is no process of considering the literal interpretation, then rejecting it and looking for a non-literal interpretation. The hearer accepts the first interpretation to yield adequate contextual effects for the minimal rationally expected effort. The first accessible interpretation in the case of metaphor should be the less than literal one, given the context in which the utterance is processed. Thus if somebody in the middle of an argument shouts 'You pig!' to his interlocutor, the first interpretation should be of 'pig' as somebody unpleasant, rather than of 'pig' as an animal.

Sperber and Wilson's analysis also accounts for Lakoff and Johnson's observation that metaphors reflect the way humans think and perceive things, so that metaphors need not be universal. Interpretive resemblance is context-dependent, and metaphors which are based on it inherently depend on contextual assumptions. These may vary from language to language. Moreover, Sperber and Wilson's account does not preclude the possibility explored by Lakoff and Johnson that the language of thought is metaphorical.

METAPHORS IN ADVERTISING

It is not difficult to see why metaphors may be attractive to advertisers. By producing a metaphorical utterance, the advertiser invites his audience to process the utterance. In so doing, the audience is made to see resemblances between the promoted product or service and the object or property featured in the metaphor. Furthermore, the audience takes part of the responsibility in deriving further assumptions about the object which it associates with the product or service. Metaphors thus play an important role in the language of advertising in both Britain and Japan, and, unlike puns, they seem to enjoy a kind of respectability.

Metaphors used in advertising are often 'conventional' or 'dead' metaphors. The following financial examples (*What Investment Magazine*, September 1992) illustrate this point:

(8) More in your PEP, not in our pockets. (Scottish Equitable)

(9) Cut out the dealing charges on your investment. (Fidelity Investment)

(10) Regular savings build up to a big sum. (Save & Prosper)

(11) Flemings . . . offer a strong performance record. (Flemings)

(12) How can a private investor get into emerging markets without going there? (The Association of Investment Trust Companies)

Indeed, it is possible that the advertisers of (8) to (12) would claim that they mean exactly what they say and that there is nothing metaphorical about their captions.

These metaphors also illustrate Lakoff and Johnson's notion of 'conceptual systems'. Thus (8) and (9) can be said to be based on the following 'structural' metaphors:

SAVING SCHEMES ARE CONTAINERS/
POSSESSION IS HAVING SOMETHING IN
ONE'S POCKET.

(8) More *in* your PEP, not *in* our *pockets*.

CHARGES/INVESTMENTS ARE OBJECTS.

(9) *Cut out* the dealing charges *on* your investment.

90

Example (10) can be said to reflect the following 'orientational' metaphor:

MORE IS UP; LESS IS DOWN.
(10) Regular savings build *up* to a big sum.

Examples (11) and (12) can be said to reflect the following ontological metaphors:

FINANCIAL ACTIVITIES ARE PERFORMING.
(11) Flemings . . . offer a *strong performance record.*

FINANCIAL ACTIVITIES ARE MARKETS.
(12) How can a private investor get into *emerging markets* without *going there?*

Similar metaphors can be discerned in Japanese advertisements, such as the following examples reflecting the ontological metaphor SKIN CARE IS WAR:

(13) a *Suhada*   *no*   *kenkoo* *to*   *anzen* *o*
natural skin   of   health and safety ACC
kangae-ta   *seihin*   *ga*
consider-PERF product NOM
Kizutsuki-yasui   *josei*   *no hada* *o*
wound-susceptible women of skin ACC
mamorimasu. (Acseine)
defend

(Our) product which has taken into consideration the health and safety of natural skin will protect vulnerable women's skin.

   b *Motto* *kakujitsu-ni*   *shigai-sen*   *o*
more   decisive-ADV ultraviolet-ray ACC
fusegimas-hoo. (Clinique)
ward off-let's

Let's ward off ultraviolet rays more decisively.

   c *Kyooteki*   *UV*   *yabur-eru.* (Kao)
powerful enemy UV   beat-PASS

The powerful enemy UV (ultraviolet rays) is beaten.

   d *Natsu*   *no* *hada* *no* *dameeji* *taisaku.* (Guerlain)
summer of skin of damage counter-measure

A counter-measure against damage for summer skin.

e *Sukinkea wa   mohaya   mamori   kara   semeru jidai.*
skin care TOP already defence from attack age
Sowan Fondamantaru   wa   24   jikan   anata
Soin   Fondamental   TOP 24 hours you
no hada no rooka   to   tatakaimasu. (Givenchy)
of skin of ageing with fight

Skin care has now moved to the age of attacking from that of defending.
Soin Fondamental will fight the ageing of your skin for 24 hours.

A caption for the Legal & General insurance company (Kleinman, 1990: No. 132) provides an illustration of the way in which a fairly creative metaphor is used in advertising:

(14) For vigorous growth, plant your money with us.

This caption is accompanied by a series of three illustrations. The first one depicts a human hand sowing seeds in the ground. The seed bag has 'umbrellas' written on it and it is covered with pictures of colourful umbrellas. The second illustration shows what appear to be green plants emerging from the ground, but, on closer inspection, they turn out to be small furled umbrellas. The third illustration shows a number of larger and colourful umbrellas coming out of the ground. The multi-coloured umbrella is the company logo of Legal & General (see Figure 5.1).

The audience, on reading (14), will search through their encyclopaedic knowledge of words such as 'growth' and 'plant' for a number of assumptions about these words. With the aid of the illustrations, the audience will remember that planting something is leaving something in the ground, that planting is followed by yield, and that a small seed may grow into a big plant. When (14) is processed against this context, it will yield a couple of fairly strong implicatures as follows:

(15) a Leave your money with Legal & General if you want it to increase steadily.
      b Invest money with Legal & General if you want a big return.

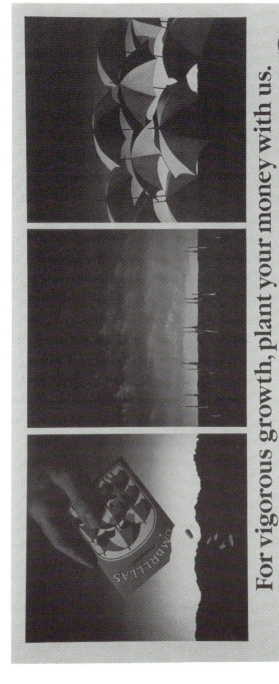

Plate 5.1 Legal & General

However, the speaker could not have intended to communicate (15a) and (15b) alone, for in that case he would have used a more direct utterance, requiring less processing effort, such as:

(16) For a big return, invest your money with Legal & General.

Additional contextual effects may outweigh the extra processing effort caused by caption (14), such as:

(17) a Investment takes time to yield a return.
b Investment requires a steady effort.
c Investment requires patience.
d Investment requires a long-term view.
e Investment requires a certain expertise.
f Investment with Legal & General will lead to something attractive.
g Investment with Legal & General will develop in a natural and reliable way.

The optimal relevance of (14) is achieved by inferring weak implicatures which are derived from the encyclopaedic information about words such as 'growth' and 'plant', implications which may vary from hearer to hearer. It is possible that some addressees had never before thought of investing money in terms of planting seeds, but, in pursuit of optimal relevance, they must see the resemblance between the two in order to derive contextual effects from the caption. The bright colours of the umbrellas may also suggest attractive results, while the umbrellas themselves carry notions of protection, insurance cover, and saving for a rainy day.

It may be a further advantage for the advertiser that the audience is invited to recover assumptions partly on its own responsibility. In the examples above, (15a) and (15b) will be fairly strongly communicated, whereas (17a) to (17g) will be weakly communicated, thus leaving the hearer to take a larger responsibility for recovering the interpretation. The advertiser can, if necessary, deny that he intended to communicate such assumptions and by involving the audience in the advertisement its attention is retained for longer.

METAPHORS IN PERFUME ADVERTISEMENTS

Perfume advertising is particularly characterised by the use of metaphor, and this perhaps derives from the special character-istics of fragrance. Sperber (1984: 115) argues that the mechanism of olfactive representation is unique. Although there are terms and expressions which describe odours, he points out that 'they almost always do so in terms of their causes and their effects'. Smells described according to cause include 'the smell of incense', 'the smell of coffee' and 'an animal smell', while examples of odours described according to their effects are 'a nauseating smell', 'a heady perfume' and 'an appetising smell'. Smells are recognisable, but not recollectable, so that when one tries to recall a smell, one conjures up a visual image associated with it:

> If I wish to recall the smell of a rose, it is in fact a visual image that I invoke; a bouquet of roses under my nose; and in the same way I will recall a church that smelled of incense, a pillow that kept the scent of patchouli, and I will almost have the impression that I sense that scent – a misleading impression, however, which will fade as soon as, relinquishing the recollection of the object it emanated from, I try mentally to reconstitute the scent itself.
>
> (Sperber 1984: 117)

It is worth noting that Sperber, being French and familiar with Catholic churches, talks of incense being associated with a church, whereas a Scot would be unlikely to make this associ-ation. The October 1992 British edition of *Elle* magazine carries a feature entitled 'Beauty Update' in which it is suggested that for most people it is the smell of cedar wood which evokes the smell of a church.

The aspect of fragrance which makes it necessary for a visual image to be used in evoking a smell may explain why adver-tisers for perfume tend to use strong visual images, as discussed in relation to Britain by Tarlo (1986). However, this goes beyond the limits of this book.

These characteristics of smell may also explain why so many advertisements for perfume employ little or no linguistic mess-age to accompany a visual image. There are simply too few expressions which are adequate to describe the fragrances being promoted. Company and product names are often the only written part of the advertisement. When there is a linguistic message in a perfume advertisement it is often written in French, regardless of the language or languages spoken in the country in which the advertisement appears (see discussion in Chapter 3 on covert communication).

When there are linguistic messages in perfume advertisements, they tend to be metaphorical, as in the following example used by Tarlo (1986: No. 29)

(18) Dangerous, but worth the risk. (Niki de Saint Phalle)

Assuming that the utterance in (18) is a statement about the perfume in question, the words 'dangerous' and 'risk' are not used to describe a state of affairs. It is clear, for example, that the caption is not claiming that the perfume is carcinogenic. There is no reason for the audience to interpret (18) literally. Rather, they are encouraged to see a resemblance between the utterance used and the thought expressed. An addressee may recover some of the following assumptions:

(19) a The perfume will attract men.
　　 b The perfume will help you have a relationship with a man.
　　 c The relationship which the perfume will help to bring may be hurtful, but it will be rewarding.

The audience might recover further assumptions, especially as the rather shadowy illustration shows a naked man and woman embracing, possibly even copulating. The name of the perfume itself might be suggestive of sexuality, as 'Phalle' could easily bring 'phallus' to mind. The audience should remember that sexual adventure is associated with 'danger', and this could lead them to:

(20) a This perfume will lead you to sexual adventure.
　　 b This perfume will bring you sexual pleasure.

In the search for optimal relevance, that is for adequate contextual effects for no unjustifiable processing effort, the audience are forced to establish the resemblance between the utterance in (18) and the thought about the perfume in question. Moreover, the audience will have to take much of the responsibility for deriving interpretations (20a) and (20b).

The notion that perfume has a seductive effect on men is commonly conveyed by metaphors in British advertising, as in the following example:

(21) Tabu, the 'forbidden' perfume by Dana. (Tabu, Dana)

There is a pun in the name of the perfume in (21), and the audience would recover 'taboo' on seeing the advertisement. The mention of 'forbidden' in the caption and the accompanying illustration of a man and woman embracing would help one to make this association. The word 'forbidden' is used less than literally, as the quotation marks would help the audience to appreciate, for there are no laws or regulations which ban the perfume. The metaphor of forbidden perfume, together with the name of the perfume and the illustration, would encourage the audience to associate the perfume with forbidden relationships. Thus, the audience would derive some assumptions about an illicit affair.

The following example employs the metaphor of seduction:

(22) A seductive gathering of lush fruits and sumptuous flowers . . . (KL, Lagerfeld)

According to the *Collins English Language Dictionary* (1987:1307), the word 'seductive' can be used in the following ways:

1   Something that is seductive is very attractive or tempting in some way.
2   If someone, especially a woman, is seductive, they are very attractive sexually.

The word 'seductive' in (22) is thus ambiguous. It is used literally in the sense that the perfume is attractive and tempts the audience to buy it. It is also used metaphorically to indicate its power of sexual attraction. The word lush may also have slight erotic overtones. By extending the context and adding the premise (23), the audience might derive the conclusion (24):

(23) If you wear something sexually attractive, you become sexually attractive yourself.
(24) If you wear the perfume in question, you become sexually attractive.

Another example of the seduction metaphor is as follows:

(25) Tempt Fate.
  It entices. Seduces. It will never go unnoticed. (Gala, Loewe)

The first utterance in (25) seems to be both urging the addressee to tempt fate by purchasing and wearing the perfume in question, and also suggesting that she tempt fate by having an illicit liaison. Against this background, the audience can derive from the rest of (25) the following, which is marked by a form of hyperbole or exaggeration:

(26) You will entice. You will seduce. You will never go unnoticed.

These examples are probably not creative metaphors, in that the association between perfume and seduction is common and widespread. It is thus easily accessible to the audience, who would be expected to derive a relatively narrow range of strong assumptions from the advertisements. However, even if the audience was not familiar with the association between perfume and seduction, it would have to make the association in processing these captions, if it were to derive adequate contextual effects.

Metaphors are also popular in Japanese advertising for perfume, as in (27) to (30):

(27) *Kiyorakana, hajimari no   yokan.* (Diorissimo, Christian Dior)
  pure   beginning of presentiment

  A pure presentiment of beginning.

(28) *Doga no   egaku 'Odori-ko'   no yooni kaoru.* (Eau de Gucci)
  Degas NOM paint 'dancing-girl' of as   smell

  As fragrant as 'The Dancer' painted by Degas.

(29) *Kaoru   hikari ga   aru-to   iu.* (Sacre, Caron)
  be fragrant light   NOM exist-COM say

  They say that there is a light which is fragrant.

(30) *Shandukuuru.   Soshite kokoro ga   utai-dasu.* (Chant du Coeur)
  Chant du Coeur and   heart NOM sing-start

  Chant du Coeur. And the heart starts singing.

However, the striking thing about Japanese perfume advertisements is that they appear to eschew metaphors of seduction, recalling Lakoff and Johnson's contention (1980) that metaphors are often specific to languages and cultures. Caption (27) does not suggest the beginning of an illicit affair, as the perfume is described as 'pure'. Caption (28) refers to the famous painting of a ballet dancer by Degas. In Japan there is an association between ballet and innocence, because some famous ballets have innocent heroines in them, and between ballet and high culture. Caption (29) refers to the perfume in question as 'a fragrant light' which contrasts with darkness suggested by the advertisements above. Caption (30) says that the perfume in question makes the heart sing. The bright colours used in the illustration suggest that it is a happy song and not a sad song of an illict affair.

The following caption seems at first sight as though it might be an exception, with a clear suggestion of lust.

(31) *Hime-rare-ta*   *yasei.* (Panthère de Cartier)
hide-PASS-PERF wildness

Hidden wildness

However, the illustration shows a perfume bottle and there is no further written message to associate the caption with seduction. Moreover, the word *yasei* (wildness) in Japanese advertising is regularly used for Western fashion, often for prestigious European brands, such as Yves Saint Laurent and Cartier. Unlike in Britain, the word does not appear to have sexual associations in Japanese usage (Tanaka 1993b).

Japanese advertisers believe that it is 'Westerness' and prestige which will sell perfume. This is reflected in a special feature on Yves Saint Laurent in the July 1992 edition of the Japanese magazine *25ans.* It promotes its brands of perfume by saying: 'In European and American societies, "fragrance" means status'. It thus emphasises the association between perfume, the West and social status.

The difference in approaches may be apprehended when the same advertisement appears in each country with subtle variations. An advertisement for Coco, made by Chanel, seems to be identical at first sight. The minimalist caption, in French in the British magazine and in *kana* in the Japanese magazine, reads 'Coco, the spirit of Chanel'. The illustration shows a scantily clad girl sitting on top of a dimly perceived flight of steps clutching an oversized bottle of Coco. In the British magazine the girl has red hair, the colour of the 'flaming temptress', and the mesh on her tights stands out. She is brought close to the addressee by the size of the photograph and by making the steps hardly visible. In the Japanese version, in contrast, the girl has demure blonde hair and a less visible mesh to her tights. She looks generally more 'virginal', and she is set back further by the smaller size of the photograph. The clearly visible steps emphasise the distance between her and the viewer.

A similar difference in the employment of metaphors can be seen in the theme of nostalgia. British advertisements often resort to nostalgic metaphors. The idea that fragrance brings back happy memories is exploited in:

(32) *Le parfum des instants précieux.* (Trésor, Lancôme)
      The perfume of precious moments.

The use of the French language and the choice of words, which remain close enough to English for the average British consumer to understand, might suggest an association with Marcel Proust's famous novel, *In Search of Lost Time*. This association may be strengthened by the name of the perfume, which means 'treasure' in English. This could bring to mind ideas of precious objects which have long been buried but have kept their attraction.

Metaphors of nostalgia seem to be absent in Japanese advertisements, which tend to stress that women should look for happiness instead. The same perfume as that described in (32) is advertised in Japan with an identical illustration (see Plate 5.2), showing the same photograph of Isabella Rossellini, with a perfume bottle and the company logo. The caption is in Japanese, although advertisers often use French captions for perfume in Japan, and the words are quite different:

(33) *Shiawase   ni   kagayaku kaori,   Trésor.*
      happiness with shine   fragrance Trésor

      The perfume which shines with happiness, Trésor.

There may also be a rather different play on the name of the perfume, with treasure suggesting brilliance and wealth, although it is unlikely that many Japanese would have access to

Plate 5.2 Lancôme

this. This perfume was the one most requested by men to give as a Christmas present to a woman in 1991, suggesting that the advertising campaign was highly successful (*JJ*, July 1992: 108).

Lancôme is not alone in preferring metaphors of happiness to those of nostalgia in Japanese advertisements, as can be seen from the following caption for Amarige, which is made by Givenchy:

(34) Amarige (in Latin characters)
      Shiawase no inryoku.
      Anata wa shinjiru-deshoo-ka.
      Kaori ni shiawase o hikiyoseru
      Chikara ga arukoto o.
      Sore wa, Givenchy ga umidashi-ta
      Atarashii shinwa.
      Hohoemi, kiboo,
      Afureru yorokobi, jun'ai, kekkon...
      Shiawase ni yukari no aru
      Hanabana o atsume-te tsukurare-ta,
      Koofuku no essensu.
      Tada yosoou tame no koosui dewa naku,
      Kooun no chaamu toshite
      Tsune-ni anata o shukufuku-suru-koto-deshoo.
      Shiawase o yobu
      <Amarige> tanjoo!

This can be translated thus:

(35) Amarige.
      The gravitational pull of happiness.
      Would you believe it?
      This perfume has a power to attract happiness.
      It is a new mythology
      Created by Givenchy.
      Smile, hope,
      Overflowing joy, pure love, marriage...
      It is the essence of happiness
      Created by collecting flowers
      Which are all associated with happiness.
      It is not a perfume merely for dressing up.
      As a lucky charm,
      It will always bless you.

Drawing happiness to you
<Amarige> is born!

Metaphors of good fortune, happiness, love and marriage abound here, rather than any associated with seduction and nostalgia. The British campaign of Amarige used no linguistic message. According to a public relations person at British Givenchy, the company has never used the association between their perfume and love and marriage. But she added that one can derive notions of love and marriage from the brand name Amarige, which could be read as a combination of the two terms in French, namely *amour* and *mariage*. This British approach contrasts with that of Givenchy in Japan, which not only used such notions as love, happiness and marriage in its advertising, but also ran a promotion campaign entitled 'Shiawase no "original pin broochi" presento' (free gift: 'original pin brooch' of happiness) (*An An*, 13 November 1992).

The reasons for this preference for metaphors of happiness are set out in the July 1992 edition of the Japanese magazine *JJ*, which carried a feature on fragrances entitled '*Sho-ka no furegurance paatii*' (The early summer fragrance party). It points to a trend which it associates particularly with Trésor and Amarige perfumes (my translation):

> The image of women in the nineties. The key word is 'happiness'. That's why sweet fragrances are popular. It is loveable women who invite happiness, rather than mysterious or individualistic women.

The feature emphasises a specific kind of happiness, linked to being 'sweet' and 'loveable'. It is no good being 'mysterious', and perhaps, by association, 'sexy', as many British advertisements recommend. Nor is it any good to be 'individualistic', a characteristic which is often associated with independence. Japanese women in the nineties do not want to be a mistress or an independent career woman. They want to be happy in marriage, and expensive foreign perfumes are there to help them to achieve this goal. Japanese advertisements therefore associate perfume with marital bliss. Notions about Japanese women which emerge from advertising are explored further in Chapter 6.

METAPHORS AND PUNS

The effects of puns involve the contrast between two or more 'chunks' (Sperber and Wilson 1986a: 88) of information, containing related concepts, whereas interpreting a metaphor involves dealing with a single chunk of information. Metaphors consist of a single expression, which offers a wide range of weak implicatures. The effect of a metaphor lies in the condensation of multiple related meanings within a single expression.

Consider the following example of a pun in a perfume advertisement

> (36) What makes a shy girl get Intimate? (Intimate, Revlon)

The addressee is expected to access (37) and then reject it for (38):

> (37) What makes a shy girl become intimate?
> (38) What makes a shy girl buy Intimate perfume?

The addressee has to process more than one 'chunk' of meaning triggered by the word, 'intimate', and the success of the pun depends on having access to these different schemata. The effect of the pun involves the contrast between two chunks, that of intimacy and that of the perfume advertised.

A second difference between puns and metaphors lies in the fact that metaphors convey an indeterminate range of thoughts, whereas puns depend on the contrast between two fairly clearly defined interpretations, linked only by similarities in sound. A creative metaphor communicates a wide range of implicatures, while a pun may communicate as little as a single one. A pun necessarily triggers two or more interpretations, which contrast with each other, but these interpretations are not usually indeterminate.

Thirdly, the intended implicature of a pun is likely to be strongly communicated, whereas the contextual effects of a metaphor are relatively weakly communicated, especially in the case of a creative metaphor. This said, standardised metaphors tend to communicate a narrower range of stronger contextual effects.

Puns and metaphors are independent of each other, but they are not mutually exclusive. An expression can be both a pun and a metaphor, and, as noted by Sacks (1974), puns often occur in metaphorical expression, as in the following perfume advertisements:

(39) A brilliant, fresh burst of fragrance from Chanel. (Cristalle, Chanel)
(40) White Linen. The crisp, refreshing fragrance to live in all year long. (White Linen, Estee Lauder)

'Brilliant', 'fresh' and 'burst of' in (39) and 'crisp', 'refreshing' and 'to live in' in (40) are used metaphorically. At the same time, both captions involve a pun based on the brand name. 'Cristalle' in (39) triggers the meaning 'crystal', especially as 'brilliant' is an adjective more commonly associated with crystal than with perfume. Similarly, 'white linen' in (40) can be interpreted in the sense of cloth, and the whiteness and crispness of linen cloth are both stereotypical notions. Thus, (39) and (40) give rise to (41) and (42), respectively:

(41) A brilliant crystal.
(42) A crisp, refreshing linen cloth, which is pleasant to live in all year round.

Each of the interpretations (41) and (42) give rise to further contextual effects, such as the beauty of a crystal and the comfort of linen, which are all extra rewards for processing the pun.

While puns and metaphors work in different ways, their utility to advertisers is similar, especially in attracting and retaining attention. The advertiser assumes that his audience has a low attention level for his kind of message, and he therefore deploys a variety of devices to overcome this problem, including puns and metaphors. Attention is retained by treating an audience as potentially creative and resourceful. Thus some puns require a considerable trawl through the audience's encyclopaedic knowledge, while some creative metaphors place great responsibility on the audience to derive weak implicatures. The notion that an audience wants advertisements to be entertaining contributes greatly to the use of puns and metaphors. An article entitled 'So it makes people laugh, but do they buy?' (*The Independent* 6 March 1991) attributes the tendency to make advertisements entertaining to the fact that audiences today are 'bombarded' with so much communicated information, including many advertisements. The advertiser does not usually aim to transfer his ultimate message by directly communicating a single, strong message. Instead, he often communicates an impression about the product or the company, which he aims to reinforce in subsequent advertisements (Jones 1986: 229–35).

CONCLUSION

Sperber and Wilson argue that the style which the speaker chooses reveals the kind of relationship which he envisages between himself and his audience:

> From the style of communication it is possible to infer such things as what the speaker takes to be the hearer's cognitive capacities and level of attention, how much help or guidance she is prepared to give him in processing her utterance, the degree of complicity between them, their emotional closeness or distance. In other words, a speaker not only aims to enlarge the mutual cognitive environment she shares with the hearer; she also assumes a certain degree of mutuality, which is indicated, and sometimes communicated by her style.
>
> (Sperber and Wilson 1986a: 217–18)

From the discussion of linguistic devices such as pun and metaphor, there appear to be some assumptions which advertisers hold about their audiences, especially their level of attention, knowledge of the world and processing abilities. Advertisers do not take it for granted that audiences have a high attention level. They use non-linguistic and linguistic devices to draw their attention. Pun and metaphor are two of the linguistic devices which advertisers in Britain and Japan frequently exploit in order to attract attention, even though it has been suggested that these devices, particularly the pun, may not be universally popular. Advertisers also treat their audiences as potentially creative and resourceful, once they have managed to gain their attention. Thus, some puns and metaphors require a search through the audience's encyclopaedic knowledge, extension of context, and considerable imaginative effort.

This may be at least partly explained by the discovery that the audience want advertisements to be entertaining or pleasurable (Cook 1992: 225), which may itself be attributable to the great volume of advertisements to which today's audiences are subjected. Puns may have humorous effects and metaphors can give aesthetic pleasure, and this accounts for the use of this style by advertisers.

6

IMAGES
OF WOMEN

INTRODUCTION

The image of women in advertising has been the subject of a vast literature in various disciplines, and this chapter aims to contribute to the debate with the aid of Relevance Theory. What follows is not a systematic sociological study, but merely an attempt to see how language is extended and altered by advertisers. Nevertheless it is hoped that, in the process, some light will be shed on the social position of women, especially in Japan.

The focus is on the ways in which the meanings of certain key words and concepts are extended and altered in advertisements which target women. The Relevance concepts of 'loose talk' and 'loose understanding' are employed for this purpose. 'Intelligence', 'individualism' and 'feminism' are three words frequently used in relation to women in advertising, and they have been chosen to illustrate the process. This chapter concentrates on what these words communicate in advertisements, and how. The social values revealed by this analysis are also explored.

Examples have been culled mainly from Japanese monthly magazines for young women, such as *J.J.*, *Can.Can*, *More*, *With*, *Cosmopolitan*, and *25 ans*, between September 1984 and November 1992. Their British equivalents, such as *Cosmopolitan*, *Vogue*, *Elle*, and *New Women*, have also been used. These Japanese magazines all have Western titles, and this reflects a strong cultural influence from the West. Nevertheless, the use of the three key words is not directly derived from Western usage.

WORD MEANING AND CONCEPTS

There seems to be general agreement among linguists that the meaning of a word can be analysed in terms of an associated concept (Fodor 1977; Kempson 1977; Lyons 1977). The classical view, known as componential analysis (Katz and Fodor 1963), is that the meaning of a word is a complex concept made up of simpler concepts. Word meaning is provided by a definition, which expresses the necessary and sufficient conditions that an object has to meet if the word is to apply to it. According to this approach, the word 'bachelor' would mean ADULT AND MALE AND HUMAN AND UNMARRIED. But Sperber and Wilson (1986a: 91) note that words such as 'bachelor' are exceptional in being treatable in this way, and that the meaning of many words cannot be analysed according to componential analysis.

Labov (1973) argues that there are no clear-cut boundaries between the meanings of words, and Lakoff (1971) refers to concepts as 'fuzzy'. The meaning of a word is an inherently indeterminate concept, so that it may not always be possible to tell whether an object satisfies it or not. Hence, there is no point in asking whether a container that seems to fall somewhere between being a cup, a mug, a bowl and a vase is really any one of them. Rather, any of these concepts can accommodate the container as a marginal case, even though the container's level of 'cuppiness' or 'mugginess' is low. The advantage of the notion of fuzzy concepts over that of well-defined classificatory concepts is that it covers a wider range of data than the latter can possibly cover.

Other linguists see the meaning of a word as a simple un-analysable concept, whose relation to other concepts is shown by 'meaning postulates' (Carnap 1956) or inference rules. In this approach, the word 'bachelor' would express the simple concept BACHELOR, with inference rules showing that propositions about bachelors entail propositions about unmarried adult human males (Fodor, Fodor and Garrett 1975; Fodor 1981). Sperber and Wilson (1986a: 91) prefer this meaning postulate approach to componential analysis.

The meaning postulate approach is compatible with, but does not entail, the fuzzy meaning approach. The meaning of a word can be a fuzzy concept which can be partially analysed in terms of meaning postulates. Sperber and Wilson's (1986a: 90) main claim is that there is no single format for the analysis of word meanings and that different words may have meanings of different types. What follows from this suggestion is that some words may be classificatory and others may be fuzzy. Although they accept that some concepts may be fuzzy, Sperber and Wilson argue that many existing arguments for fuzziness fail to distinguish between words that are strictly defined but loosely used, and words whose meanings are genuinely fuzzy. Thus Sperber and Wilson (1986b: 165) see the word 'bald' as strictly defined but loosely used. The 'baldness paradox' is that one accepts that a man with no hair is bald, and also that a man with one hair is bald. 'Via the general principle that if a man with n hairs is bald then a man with $n + 1$ hairs is bald', one comes to the conclusion that a man with a full head of hair is bald. Sperber and Wilson offer a solution to this paradox by accepting that 'bald' is a strictly defined classificatory concept, with the necessary and sufficient condition, of having no hair. Thus to describe a man with one hair as bald is strictly speaking false. But many utterances which are strictly speaking false are none the less pragmatically appropriate, and the use of 'bald' to apply to a man with very little hair would fall into this category. The more hair the person has, the less acceptable the loose use will be, to a point where it is not acceptable at all. Thus the point at which looseness becomes unacceptable is dependent on context.

The problems analysed in this chapter go well beyond the 'fuzziness' of words in their literal meaning, even though Sperber and Wilson would probably treat 'intelligence', 'individualism' and 'feminism' as fuzzy (Wilson, personal communication; Sperber 1988). In the advertisements examined below, these words are used in ways which clearly go beyond their standard meanings, whether these meanings are classificatory or fuzzy. To say that a concept is fuzzy is not to say that it can be stretched indefinitely. The concepts dealt with in this chapter are stretched beyond normal fuzziness of meaning, to the point of an over-extension of meaning.

The ways in which the meanings of words may be overextended depend on the notion that the meaning of a word is provided by an associated concept. According to Sperber and Wilson (1986a: 86), a concept holds three distinctive types of information: logical, encyclopaedic and lexical. The logical entry for a concept is a set of deductive rules. These deductive rules apply to logical forms of which the concept is a constituent, and thus determine its analytic implications. For example, the logical entry for the concept 'elephant' would indicate that it is an animal. The encyclopaedic entry for a concept consists of information about the extension of the concept. This type of information helps to determine the contextual implications of the concept. The encyclopaedic entry for the concept 'elephant', for example, would include assumptions about its tusks and trunk. Finally, the lexical entry of a concept contains information about its counterpart in natural language. The lexical entry of the concept 'elephant' would contain information about the words 'elephant' in English and *zoo* in Japanese.

Over-extension of meaning is not related to problems of translation. It is true that the Japanese words *chisei, chiteki, kosei,* and *kosei-teki* cannot always be translated by the English words 'intelligence', 'intelligent', 'individuality' and 'individualistic', respectively. But these 'translation gaps' are irrelevant for our purposes. The ways in which these Japanese words are used are special in terms of Japanese usage, and this cannot be accounted for on the grounds that English words do not match those in Japanese.

INTELLIGENCE

The words *chisei* (intelligence) and *chiteki* (intelligent) have become ubiquitous in Japanese advertisements which target young women, but it would be premature to conclude that Japanese society is changing and that intelligent women are now accepted and encouraged. On the contrary, intelligence is still regarded as a desirable quality for men rather than for women in Japan (Smith 1987: 11).

This apparent paradox is resolved by the fact that the words *chisei* (intelligence) and *chiteki* (intelligent), when applied to women, are used in an extremely restricted and strange way. This can be seen from the following examples:

(1)   *Chiteki-de*   *joohinna shiruku burausu.* (Tokyo Blouse)
      intelligent-COP noble   silk   blouse

      An intelligent and noble silk blouse.

110

(2) *Chotto ereganto-de   chotto   interijensuna*
a bit   elegant-COP a bit   intelligent
inshoo   ga   shinsen. (Paco Rabanne)
impression NOM refreshing

The impression of being a little elegant and a little intelligent is refreshing.

(3) *Feminin-shikku o   beesu   ni*
feminine-chic ACC base   on
chitekina   kaori   o   tadayowa-seru. (Pop International)
intelligent feeling ACC   float-CAUS

Using a feminine and chic style as a base, you let the feeling of being intelligent float.

(4) *Chisei   to   yasei.   San   Rooran   no*
Intelligence and wildness.   Saint Laurent of
ganchiku. (Yves Saint Laurent)
suggestion

Intelligence and wildness. Saint Laurent's suggestion.

(5) *Utsukushisa wa   chisei   no jiko-shuchoo.* (Elegance)
beauty   TOP intelligence of self-assertion

Beauty is (the manifestation of) intelligence asserting itself.

These advertisements for fashion goods are effectively suggesting that women should express their intelligence through their clothes and handbags. Intelligence is no more than a superficial quality which clothes and accessories give to a woman. It is desirable for a woman to be intelligent in her choice of clothes, but women are not encouraged to be intelligent in a general sense. Intelligence describes appearance rather than mental capacity, and seems closer in its meaning to words such as 'elegance', 'femininity', or 'sophistication', than to words like 'brightness' and 'cleverness', which a thesaurus would suggest as synonyms.

A feature in *J.J.* (October 1986) entitled 'Suggestions for intelligent elegance' *(Chiteki eregansu no teian)* pushes the argument further (my translation):

a In choosing a dress . . . (remember that) 50 per cent of

the creation of an impression of intelligence depends on your neck-line. An appropriate round neck and golden buttons are the key to success.

b The main trend of this year's suits is towards those which have a tightly shaped waist . . . a tight waist-line leads to an expression of intelligence.

c You cannot omit black, for it is a front runner for an intelligent-looking colour.

This tells us that an 'intelligent' woman wears a black dress with a round neck and a tight waist-line, with golden buttons. But there is no inherent reason why a round neck should be more 'intelligent' than a V-neck. Nor is it self-evident why a small waist, the colour black, and gold buttons should be associated with 'intelligence'. The point is simply that all these features were in fashion at the time that the feature was written.

'Intelligent elegance' is pragmatically questionable, but another example drawn from an advertisement for a Volkswagen car is pragmatically unacceptable in its literal form:

(6)   *Chiteki   eregansu. Jetta.*
      intelligent elegance Jetta
      Chitekina   machi o   chitekina   josei   to
      intelligent town ACC intelligent woman with
      Chiteki-ni   hashirimasu. (Volkswagen)
      intelligent-ADV drive

      Intelligent elegance. Jetta.
      It drives through an intelligent town with an intelligent woman.
      In an intelligent manner.

Only 'intelligent woman' is well-formed, whereas 'intelligent town' and 'the car drives in an intelligent manner' can only be used metaphorically. Intelligence is used to express a quality which is not exactly to do with intellect, but which in some way resembles being intelligent. The background to the advertisement is a French restaurant, so that intelligence again seems to be synonymous with 'fashionable', since that is how France is generally regarded by the Japanese. The car advertised is German. Perhaps, German cars and French cooking are seen as *chiteki* assets of the respective countries.

The concept of intelligence is also used to imply desirability in a sexual sense. Intelligence, elegance, and appeal to men seem to be virtually interchangeable, as in this example (see Plate 6.1):

(7) *Yappari 'shiroi su-hada'   ga   sekushii-da-shi,*
     after all 'white natural-skin' NOM sexy-COP-and
     chitehi-de-sho . . . (La Este)
     intelligent-COP-FP

     After all, 'white, natural skin' is sexy and intelligent, isn't it?

Can Cam carried a feature entitled 'On (becoming) a "desirable woman" (*'Ii onna' e no henshin sengen*) (December 1987). The suggestions made there overlap almost completely with *J.J.*'s definition of 'intelligent elegance', including the colour black, a small waist and golden buttons. Furthermore, one of the three cars listed as 'Cars for a "desirable woman" ' is Volkswagen's Jetta, mentioned above, for the very reason that it is 'intelligent-looking'.

An explicit connection between intelligence and knowledge is certainly made in an advertising campaign run by Kanebo, the second largest cosmetics company in Japan, but knowledge is defined in such a way as to marginalise it. 'Intelligence' (in English) was the catch-phrase for its Morphe brand in the following captions:

(8) Intelligence. (in English)
     Sore ga   kimi no utsukushisa.
     that NOM you of beauty
     Kite-iru   fuku   ni chisei   o   kanjiru.
     wear-ing clothes in intelligence ACC feel
     Tatta ippon no kuchibeni kara   mo . . .
     one one of lipstick from   even

     Intelligence. (in English)
     That is (the secret of) your beauty.
     Your intelligence is seen in your clothes.
     Even in the lipstick which you wear.

(9) Intelligence. (in English)
     Chishiki   ni   kawaku-no   wa   ii   keredo
     knowledge for thirst-NOM TOP good but
     Hada no kawaki   wa   kinmotsu desu.
     skin of dryness TOP taboo   COP

Plate 6.1 La Este

Intelligence.
It is good to thirst for knowledge, but
it is taboo to let your skin dry.

(10) Intelligence. (in English)
Haru   wa   'seibutsugaku'-teki   ni   mo   hada
spring TOP 'biology'-manner   in   also skin

ga   kappatsu-ni   narimasu-ne.
NOM active-ADV   become-FP

Intelligence. (in English)
In spring, from a biological point of view, too, the
skin is activated, isn't it?

(11) Intelligence. (in English)
Ikita   chishiki   wa   utsukushii.
alive knowledge TOP beautiful
Morufe   ga   shuchoosuru   utsukushisa, interijensu.
Morphe NOM insist   beauty   intelligence

Intelligence . . .
Living knowledge is beautiful.
The kind of beauty that Morphe insists upon, that is,
intelligence.

Caption (8) is similar to earlier examples, suggesting that a
woman's intelligence manifests itself not only in her clothes but
also in her lipstick. Caption (9), in contrast, introduces a classic
definition of intelligence as the thirst for knowledge, but only to
trivialise it immediately by suggesting that women's knowledge
is about their skin. A similar theme is taken up in (10), where
biological knowledge enables women to take care of their skin.
Caption (11) sums it all up by reducing a woman's knowledge
and intelligence to the traditional role of knowing how to make
herself look beautiful.

British advertisements employ the concept of 'intelligence' in
a similar manner. Consider this example for Elancyl taken from
Elle (British edition, October 1992):

(12) A firmer stomach or bust
Elancyl, *l'intelligence du corps*

The French text translates as 'the intelligence of the body' and
the illustration shows a scantily clad glamorous woman, with

an apparently firm bust and stomach. There is a long accompanying text in small print which uses much pseudo-scientific jargon, including words such as 'serum', 'elastin', and 'collagen'. The basic message is that a woman's intelligence has to do with knowing how to make herself presentable, as in the Japanese Morphe advertisement. More weakly, and possibly covertly, communicated is the suggestion that a woman should know how to make herself desirable for men, as in the Japanese La Este advertisement ((7) above).

Another trivialised connection with classic definitions of intelligence consists of an association with art. Thus *Can Cam*'s feature on how to be a desirable woman, mentioned above, also recommends visits to art galleries. Advertisements suggest that an 'intelligent' woman is one who wears expensive jewellery and goes to exhibitions, as in the following example:

(13) *Bijutsukan   e   iku josei   ga   fuete-imasu.*
art gallery to go women   NOM   increase-ing
Purachina   o   tsukeru josei   ga   fuete-imasu.
(Platinum Promotion Forum)
platinum   ACC   wear   women NOM increase-ing

The number of women going to art galleries is increasing.
The number of women wearing platinum is increasing.

The use of this artistic theme by advertisers is undoubtedly related to the fact that in Japan women are the prime consumers of art and culture (Moeran 1983: 101). However, culture is treated here as just another item of conspicuous consumption.

These images of women run parallel to the kind of education received by women in contemporary Japan (Hoshii 1986; Smith 1987; Condon 1991). After 1945 educational opportunities for women improved considerably. In fact, looking at the figures for boys and girls attending senior high school and college or university, it might seem that Japanese women now enjoy equal educational opportunities with men. But there is a significant difference in the type and quality of education received according to gender. Women tend to go to junior colleges, which are regarded as 'a modern version of the old schools for brides' (Smith 1987: 11). Women also tend to study 'women's subjects',

such as home economics, education, language and literature.
Japanese society has long valued women's mental qualities in the domestic domain, but contemporary advertisements in magazines for young women do not seem to apply the notion of an intelligent woman to this sphere. An ideal woman has been described since the Meiji era as *ryoo-sai-ken-bo*, that is, 'good wife, wise mother' (Smith 1987: 7). Japanese women are expected to rule the home, and it is they who are responsible for child care and the management of the household budget. They are encouraged to exercise their brains in their limited capacities as managers of households and mothers. It is possible that modern forms of the Meiji slogan could be found in magazines which aim at an older age group.

Words such as *chisei* (intelligence) and *chiteki* (intelligent) are usually, though not exclusively, employed for women in Japanese advertising, that is, they describe women in advertisements which are targeted at women. It may be that women are being seen as *chiteki* in a limited and superficial sense, even though they are not encouraged to exercise their mental ability to the full. Women are accepted as *chiteki* in their own small ways, so long as they do not cross the border and invade men's territory and threaten them. Example (14) provides support for this suggestion:

(14) *Egao   mo   onna   no chisei*
     smiling face also woman of intelligence
     kashira. (Narisu Cosmetics)
     it appears

     It appears that a smiling face is also (a manifestation of) women's intelligence.

The caption implies that there is one kind of intelligence for women and another kind for men. A smile belongs to the former, and not to the latter.

Although 'intelligence' is arguably a fuzzy concept, the use of the word in Japanese advertising cannot be wholly accounted for by the notion of fuzzy concept, and it is a straightforward case of loose use. There is some resemblance in content between what the advertisers wish to communicate and what the words *chisei* and *chiteki* express. Strictly defined, 'intelligent' means 'with mental abilities which can be applied in several directions'.

To attain the meaning used in advertising, it is necessary to add an extra premise to the context, namely that the abilities desirable in a woman are those to do with being presentable. Intelligence then means mental abilities which can be applied to being presentable. A passage in a small column on Greta Garbo in the October 1992 edition of *25 ans* (p. 64, my translation) supports this idea:

> The intelligence which understood what is beautiful, what is feminine, must have been one of her attractions.

In spite of this loose use of the word 'intelligence', the advertiser can trust the addressee to grasp the intended implications. In processing the captions, it would cause the addressee too much friction to interpret the word as meaning 'academically excellent', as there is no reason to believe that the word is being employed to communicate such implications. A stereotype of Japanese women as presentable but not intellectual would help the addressee to process the captions by giving her access to an appropriate context. Implications to do with general intellectual abilities would be suppressed, and those to do with a particular use of these abilities retained. Optimal relevance would be achieved once the implications to do with appearance were recovered.

This is a clear case of the intentional loose use of words. In Japanese advertising 'intelligent' and 'intelligence' are used deliberately in order to imply sophistication, femininity, and elegance, which are regarded as desirable qualities for women. Such qualities are good selling points from the advertiser's point of view. There is no vagueness involved, but rather a carefully crafted loose use of the term.

INDIVIDUALISM

There has long been strong emphasis on the importance of the group over the individual in Japan, and yet there has been an increasing number of advertisements in young women's magazines which emphasise *kosei* (individuality). This raises questions as to potential shifts in Japanese conceptual structures. One could even see it as part of a threat to Japanese group ideology, as discussed by Moeran (1983: 105, 1984: 262).

A closer analysis reveals that there is no threat, and that the

word *kosei* is actually being used to buttress group ideology.
Consider the following example for a Longines watch:

(15) *Watashi wa   interia-dezainaa ... Ronjin   no*
     I   TOP interior designer Longines of
     konkuesto wa ... chisei-bi   dokusoosei
     Conquest TOP intelligence beauty originality
     ni afure, kiwadatte koseiteki (Longines)
     of full   strikingly individualistic

     I am an interior designer ... Longines' Conquest is
     full of intelligent beauty and originality, and is strik-
     ingly individualistic.

On the left of the illustration there is a black and white photograph of a young European woman, presumably an interior
designer, while on the right a pair of Longines watches are
displayed in full colour. The woman is engaged in a so-called
katakana profession, that is a profession which is written in the
katakana script used for Western loan words. *Katakana* pro-
fessions are regarded as fashionable and desirable due to their
Western 'flavour'. The design of the watches is not dissimilar to
that of the Rolex 'oyster', widely regarded as prestigious and
fashionable. Individualism is clearly not being defined as having
your own style, but rather as adhering to fashion. The association with *chisei-be* (intelligent beauty) reinforces this interpretation, given my previous discussion of the use of the word
'intelligence'.

The association of individualism with fashion is equally clear
in the following example:

(16) *Itaria no ii   iro,   ii   katachi Guccini.*
     Italy of good colour good shape Guccini
     Jinsei o   koseiteki-ni   tanoshimu
     life   ACC individualistic-ADV enjoy
     josei-tachi   no tame ni (Guccini)
     woman-PL of sake for

     Good Italian colour and shape, Guccini.
     For women who enjoy their life in an individual style.

Individualism means buying tableware from Italy, which is
regarded as a country which produces high quality, fashion
goods.

The interpretation of the word *kosei-teki* (individualistic) as doing things which are fashionable is not limited to advertising. A survey carried out in 1972 (Suzuki 1975: 118–20) asked the question 'Do you think that you can achieve greater individualism by following fashion?' 61.5 per cent of women and 48.2 per cent of men answered yes to this question. While only slightly more women than men replied positively, nearly twice as many men as women answered with a clear no (41.9 per cent versus 22.9 per cent), whereas a larger number of women were undecided.

'Individualism' in advertisements appears to have strong overtones of élitism, both in terms of wealth and social standing. Advertisers seem at first sight to be endorsing the idea of 'doing one's own thing', but in practice they are advising the purchase of products which are expensive and have high status. To be individualistic is to be able to afford expensive and socially prized goods and services.

Running through most of the advertisements which refer to individualism is a strong association with Western culture. At first sight, this might seem to reflect the fact that the idea of individualism entered Japan from Western sources, but a closer examination merely shows that the West is associated with what is expensive, fashionable and socially desirable. Many of the goods and services offered by advertisers in association with 'individualism' are European in origin, coming especially from France and Italy. There is also an undertone of cultural dependence on the West, as in the following example:

(17) *Kono natsu,   jibun no kami   o*
this summer self of hai   ACC
Amerika   no onna   no ko   no yooni
America of female of child of as
Yooroppa   no onna   no ko   no yooni
European of female of child of as
Jibun   de heaa-dezain   shichaoo. (Benezel)
self   by hair-design let's do

Let's design our own hair this summer.
As American girls do.
As European girls do.

'Doing your own thing' is acceptable and desirable only to the extent that American and European girls are already doing it.

Equating 'individualism' with doing what other people do can also be related to more practical motives when 'individualism' comes to include elements of common sense. This is the advice given to young women in the magazine, *With* (July 1987) (my translation):

a This year's popular colour, green, plays an important role in emphasising individuality . . .

b You should wear a vivid-coloured polo-neck shirt to emphasise your individuality.

c Your fringe should be cut short and 'individualistic' . . .

d The key to making you look fresh and individualistic is to have your hair in an off-the-face style.

In the same issue the reader is informed that green is currently the most fashionable colour in Paris, but the other aspects of these recommendations are linked to the hot and humid Japanese summer. Vivid colours tend to be popular because in tropical conditions they reflect heat rather than absorbing it. At the same time, it is eminently sensible to keep one's hair short and off one's face at this time of year.

Even an advertisement which at first sight seems to be promoting individual choice proves to be ambivalent. This caption is for a display of wrist-watches identical except for their colour:

(18) *Watashi no iro o motte-i-nai to,*
I   of colour ACC have-ing-NEG if
hazukashii. (Casio)
embarrassing

It is embarrassing if I do not have my own colour.

The watches are all of the same model, thus choosing a colour is a social obligation enforced by loss of face. The limits to individualism, in the sense of free choice, remain immense.

It seems contradictory to use the word individualistic to mean behaving as other people do, but this seeming paradox is resolved by the notion of 'loose talk'. What is happening here is an extension of word meaning by loose usage. Individualism in its usual sense means being able to do what one wants to do. To this context is added the premise that what a woman wants is what the rest of society wants. The implications of individualism which involve each person behaving uniquely are dropped, as they do not fit with behaving as society wants and remaining inconspicuous. The assumption that advertising messages are 'positive' would also help such a comprehension process. If 'individualism' is promoted in advertising, it must mean that it is something positive and desirable, so it is unlikely to mean behaving differently from others and standing out in a crowd. Thus the philosophy of individualism is turned into behaving as the rest of society wants you to behave.

Japanese group ideology is thus rescued from the supposed threat to its existence. A 'dangerous' concept has simply been absorbed into conventional wisdom. The use of the word *kosei-teki* (individualistic) in advertisements resolves culture clash by interpreting new notions in the old context against conventional premises. This conclusion is consistent with the findings of Moeran (1984: 262) that *kosei* is not equivalent to what we know as 'individualism' in the West and that *kosei* is neatly absorbed into the Japanese way of life. The success of Japanese advertising which stresses 'individualism' would logically result in everybody behaving and dressing the same. It can thus be argued that Japanese 'groupism' is underpinned rather than threatened by the use of the concept of 'individualism' in advertising.

A straightforward notion of individualism is no more likely to be promoted in Western than in Japanese advertising, given that advertising is about selling to a mass audience. An association between 'individualism' and élitism can indeed be found in advertising in British magazines, and this is related to the Japanese examples already given. The connection between 'individualism' and élitism is illustrated by an advertisement for Citizen Watches, which appeared in *The Sunday Times* colour supplement (13 December 1987). The picture, in grey or neutral tones, shows a naked girl with a Citizen watch picked out in luminous gold on her wrist. The caption reads as follows:

(19) There is no such thing as the average Citizen.

There is a pun on the word 'citizen', which is both the brand name and an expression for a member of society. As it is written in capital letters, like the brand name, (20) would be recovered as the most accessible interpretation:

(20) There is no such thing as an average Citizen watch.

122

By adding to the context assumption (21), the audience would derive (22):

(21) An advertisement says how superior the advertised product is.
(22) A Citizen watch is better than average.

However, there is another way of reading this advertisement. The interpretation of the word 'citizen' as a member of society is encouraged by the fact that the advertisement shows a woman as well as a watch. The following interpretation is made accessible:

(23) There is no such thing as an average member of society.

The woman is naked and shows no obvious sign of social status. She is described as 'average' in height, hair colour, age and weight. Her only obvious distinguishing feature is the watch which she is wearing. Thus, it is wearing a Citizen watch which makes her a special person. Furthermore, in spite of the description of the woman as 'average', she actually has a mysterious beauty. This may suggest that special people wear Citizen watches. Thus to be 'individualistic' means to be able to afford an expensive watch, which is usually worn by beautiful and privileged people.

Loose use of the word individualism can also exploit stereotypical and negative images of women. Thus a caption for Kotex Fems Tampons reads:

(24) Fems. Doing things your way,

This is followed by the text:

(25) Kotex Fems Tampons are designed for today's woman.
The woman who chooses to do things her way.

One illustration found with the above caption shows a young woman dressed casually in a shirt and trousers. She has conspicuous pink hair, in which there is a black bow with orange dots. She has a dog of the same pink colour, with the same bow on its head (see Plate 6.2).

In interpreting (24) and (25) against this background, the audience would extend the context to the immediate visual

Plate 6.2 Fems

environment, and see this woman as 'the woman who chooses to do things her way'. The audience would be given access to a context in which women are oppressed and cannot do things their way, and therefore do not have such unconventional hair or pets. The context would also contain a premise such as the following:

(26) Dyeing your hair pink is doing things your way.

Another illustration found with this caption shows a tall office building. Out of one of its many windows comes a typewriter, apparently thrown by someone inside, breaking the window pane. The only way (24) and (25) could be relevant would be to interpret them as describing a woman who cannot be seen in the illustration, but who is throwing the typewriter out of the window. The audience would be encouraged to imagine a situation in which a woman has been working over a typewriter but has lost her temper and has thrown the thing out of the window. The audience would be encouraged to extend the context by thinking of another situation in which a woman is repressed and unable to show her temper. She would be a woman who does not do things her way. The context chosen for the interpretation of the advertisement would include a premise such as:

(27) Throwing your typewriter out of the window is doing things your way.

This advertisement apparently endorses the notion of individualism, but in reality it is peddling negative stereotypes about women. Such behaviour is not part of mature and responsible adulthood, and one does not have to be outrageous in order to be individualistic. 'Individualism' in this case merely implies doing something that other people do not do. The use of the concept has not retained other implications, such as being responsible for the consequences of one's own behaviour. The notion of individualism has been reduced to that of doing childish and silly things, which reinforces negative perceptions of women.

The notion of individualism is indeed being used to endorse stereotypes in both Britain and Japan, rather than reflecting real changes in the social position of women. Stereotypes of women help audiences to process utterances which involve the concept of individualism. Stereotypical images provide easy access to contexts which include certain assumptions about women, thus leading to the interpretations intended by advertisers.

FEMINISM IN JAPAN

This section examines a case which can be explained in terms of what Deirdre Wilson (personal communication) would call *loose understanding*. One of the situations where loose understanding may occur is where a word is borrowed by one society from another, thus resulting in a change of meaning. In this case, the Japanese loan word *feminisuto* has acquired a radically different meaning from that of the English original 'feminist'.

The following caption, used in advertisements for the company Tokyo Gas, illustrates this change of meaning. This series was so successful that it won a prestigious Asahi Advertising Prize (*Asahi Advertising Prize 1984* 1985: 60–1).

(28) *Toshi gasu-tte   feminisuto ne.* (Tokyo Gas)
city   gas-COMP feminist FP

City Gas is a feminist, isn't it?

This caption was used in a series of four different advertisements, each accompanied by a different illustration and text. The first, for a gas cooker with a special sensor, shows a large pot boiling over, and the text reads:

(29) If the flame is blown out by something boiling over, the gas will cut out.

The second advertisement (see Plate 6.3) is for a similar sensor device, and it depicts a woman wearing an apron and drying a dish with a cloth. The text reads:

(30) If imperfect combustion occurs due to lack of ventilation, this boiler will automatically turn off the gas.

The third picture is of a cocktail glass and matches, suggesting a drink at a bar. It advertises a gas meter with a micro computer, and it is accompanied by the words:

(31) Even if the gas leaks, or you forget to switch it off, or if you lose your head at the time of an earthquake, you can rest assured with Maiseefu (My Safe).

The fourth illustration depicts the reflection in a mirror of a

Plate 6.3 Tokyo Gas

woman putting on lipstick, whose attention seems to be diverted by something. An alarm for gas leaks is the subject of this advertisement, and the text is:

(32) Gas leaks and imperfect combustion will surely be detected.

The company is clearly being described as 'feminist' on the grounds that it has come up with these various ingenious devices in order to help women with their work in the kitchen. The use of the particle *ne* in (28) marks the utterance as feminine. The audience is encouraged to imagine a woman's voice praising the company for improvements in gas equipment, which help women with their household duties and make their lives safer. The word *feminisuto* is apparently used to laud a desirable quality in men, in that the company is male dominated.

It is probably the wife and mother featured in an advertising campaign from the previous year who is calling Tokyo Gas a *feminisuto*. In 1983 Tokyo Gas won a prize for advertisements promoting the same equipment, which used the following caption:

(33) *Kaasan yorokobu-daroo na.*
mother rejoice will FP

I think Mother will be pleased.

The caption accompanied five advertisements which depicted a father and a son in conversation. The sentence's final particle *na* marks masculinity. The word *kaasan* can be used by a husband referring to his wife, especially in the presence of his children. Thus (33) can be said by either the father or the son, and the audience should be able to derive (34):

(34) Mother will be pleased with the equipment.

As these devices are all produced by Tokyo Gas, the audience should have no difficulty in also deriving (35):

(35) Mother will be pleased with Tokyo Gas.

A Japanese audience would understand the use of the lone word *feminisuto*, whether or not they knew the meaning of the English word 'feminist'. It would not be necessary for them to know the meaning of the word in advance. An addressee would learn how *feminisuto* should be understood through the context in which the Japanese word was being employed. Even an addressee who knew the English word would quickly realise that the Japanese way of using it was different, not because of her previous knowledge of the English word, but in spite of it.

It seems unlikely that more than a handful of Japanese would question Tokyo Gas's attitudes towards women, even though it could be argued, from a Western perspective, that it is pure male chauvinism, rather than feminism, to assume that men should gain women's praises by improving women's kitchen equipment. According to Hoshii (1986: 80), 89 per cent of women accept that housework is women's responsibility. For them, housework is part of being a woman, just like putting on lipstick. The very concept of a feminist in the English sense is at best dimly perceived as some strange foreign idea.

The loan word *feminisuto* clearly does not mean what the original English word means, and this usage is not limited to advertising. It does not take long for British students in Japan to learn that a *feminisuto* is someone who readily opens doors for women. And yet, in Britain, radical feminists may take offence at such a gesture, which is characterised as a typical example of 'male chauvinism'. Condon (1991: 59) explains the phenomenon as follows:

> There is no Gloria Steinem in Japan. The feminist movement is so limited that even the word *feminist-o* refers not to women but to men who say, 'Ladies first'.

The Japanese usage of the word 'feminist' is exceedingly loose, to a degree made possible only by the passage of the word from one language to the other. It would be an unacceptably loose use of the word in an English-speaking community, for it contradicts too many of the logical and contextual implications of the concept. What seems to have happened is that the English word 'feminist' only retained part of its meaning when it was absorbed into Japanese, namely the part that involved being pleasant and helpful to women. This was indeed revolutionary in a society where women were still expected to serve men as their absolute lords and masters. However, the part of the concept that involved treating women on an equal footing to men was ignored. There was no clash between the way in which the word was used and people's knowledge of the word, given that it did not exist before. The Japanese meaning has thus ended up by being more contrary than similar to the original meaning.

This shift can be explained by an analysis of word meaning (Sperber and Wilson 1986a: 86). Most words express simple concepts, with logical entries which determine their analytic implications, and encyclopaedic entries which contribute to their contextual implications. When one first hears the word 'feminist', one opens a new *conceptual address,* and begins, in a gradual way, to build up the word's logical and encyclopaedic entries. Possible changes of meaning may occur in the following ways. A hearer with radically different encyclopaedic assumptions about the world may fail to notice some of the contextual implications intended by the speaker, and recover other, unintended implications which may become part of the encyclopaedic stereotype associated with the concept. Secondly, something that for the original speaker was an analytic implication, determined by a logical entry, may be perceived as a contextual implication determined by an encyclopaedic entry, and vice versa. In either case, loose understanding occurs, and as a result a change of meaning occurs. Loose interpretation is the source of much change in word meaning. It is not only foreigners who understand strange words loosely. Children understand adults loosely, that is they recover some analytic or contextual implications, but not others.

In the case of *feminisuto*, it can be argued that the Japanese-speaking hearer, holding drastically different encyclopaedic assumptions about women and their position in society, failed to retrieve a subset of implications intended by the foreign speaker, which have to do with women being independent and having equal opportunities. The hearer only recovered other implications, which have to do with being pleasant to women. This latter subset of implications may have been unintended by the speaker, but they may have been relevant and easily accessible to the hearer, because of the nature of Japanese society. The Japanese have altered the meaning by altering the implications. It could even be argued that this distortion is an indication of the fact that Japanese society was not prepared for feminist concepts.

There is much more work to be done in this area, but it is hoped that this example of the metamorphosis of the word 'feminist' has provided a sketch of how changes of word meaning can be analysed within a pragmatic framework. However, this is no more than a suggestion for a whole area which requires much further research.

CONCLUSION

In this chapter, the focus has been on a few key words used in advertisements targeted at women, and extension and shift of word meaning has been analysed in a framework based on Relevance Theory. A small set of data was chosen to exemplify different kinds of extension or change of word meaning. Crucial to the analysis of this process are the notions of 'loose talk', which involves the addition of extra premises to the context, and 'loose understanding', in which some of the contextual implications associated with the word intended by the speaker may be lost by the hearer.

The portrayal of women in Japanese society was also hinted at. Despite the frequent use of words such as 'intelligent' and 'individualistic', which suggest new images of women, a closer examination reveals the reinforcement of traditional role models. Women's 'intelligence' manifests itself in their choice of clothes and cosmetics and their sweet smile. 'Individualism' turns out to be a search for high fashion and social approval. A 'feminist' is someone who provides sophisticated kitchen gadgets for women to do their housework. Rather than reflecting any real change in the attitude to women, these words are used in ways which support and emphasise stereotypes of women (Tanaka 1990a, 1998).

The analysis has also suggested ways in which one society absorbs new notions from another. Japanese society seems to have coped with potential threats from the introduction of concepts such as individualism and feminism by interpreting them against the background of traditional values, or by removing some of the contextual implications attached to the concept which contradict conventional ideas. Thus, Japanese group ideology and male chauvinism have been rescued, and potential culture clashes have largely been avoided.

CONCLUSION

The purpose of this book has been to evaluate some of the basic assumptions of Relevance Theory, and to apply the theory to an analysis of the language used by advertisers. In so doing, I hope to have shed new light on some of the assumptions of Relevance Theory, while also contributing to an overall understanding of the style of the language of advertising. I take style to be a jigsaw puzzle, a picture consisting of numerous pieces of different shapes and colours. A particular style of writing is a complex conglomerate of various aspects of language use, related to the expectations which a communicator has of his addressee.

The heterogeneous nature of the book is the result of an attempt to analyse a recognisable style. Chapters 3 to 6 isolate for analysis some of the most striking characteristics of one particular style. Thus, Chapter 3 discusses audience manipulation through covert communication. This is contrasted with ostensive communication, which lies at the heart of Sperber and Wilson's analysis of communication. The chapter gives a prominence, not accorded by Sperber and Wilson, to a type of communication in which two involved parties are typically unequal. This is nicely complemented by Forceville (1998), in a study of the visual aspect of covert communication in advertising.

Chapter 4 examines the use of the pun in advertising. This involves considerations of ambiguity and gives an opportunity to re-examine fundamental properties of communication. Punning is at first sight problematic for Relevance Theory, in that the interpretation first triggered by an utterance is not the one intended by the communicator. However, the chapter explains how the audience rejects the first interpretation and goes on to retrieve the second interpretation, guided by the search for optimal relevance. This demonstrates that Relevance Theory provides a useful account of types of communication in which the communicator intends two or more interpretations. Chapter 5 analyses how metaphors are employed in advertisements. Relevance notions of 'loose talk' and 'weak communication' form the core of this analysis. Metaphor seems to have become a sub-genre in itself, giving rise to the speculation that, if growth continues at the current rate, the number of researchers studying metaphor will outgrow the number of people on earth by the year 2039 (Myers 1994: 134, attributed to Wayne Booth). Two recent works are especially useful complements to my book in this respect. Goatly (1997) offers a comprehensible account of metaphor based on Relevance Theory and functional linguistics, drawing some of his examples from advertising. Forceville (1998) investigates the ways in which visual, rather than verbal, metaphors are employed in advertising. His analysis is enriched by insight from a range of frameworks, in which Relevance Theory plays an important part.

Chapter 6 discusses how individual words can be used in extended ways, in one case leading to a definitive shift in word meaning. The notions of 'loose talk' and 'loose use' are vital in accounting for such usage. Sociological considerations of the status of women are important to understand why this has happened. How such considerations interact with the way in which language is used in the media needs further investigation (Tanaka 1998).

The selection of topics clearly leaves aside many other devices in the language of advertising, but nevertheless covers a wide array of theoretical and analytical problems. Metonymy and synecdoche would be just two examples of topics which would deserve further investigation (Myers 1994).

Despite the low respect which advertising is generally accorded in the intellectual world, the language of advertising provides a stimulating approach to understanding the human mind, and studies of advertising have flourished since the publication of the hardback edition of this book. Advertising, for all its crass and mercenary qualities, attracts highly qualified people, and advertisers need to keep constantly in touch with rapidly changing social realities. Advertisements give sharply focused and highly topical insights into the way in which communication works. Moreover, advertising is a particularly good medium for assessing the force of language, given the obsession of advertisers with overcoming the social barriers between themselves and their audience.

BIBLIOGRAPHY

Aitchison, J. (1987) *Words in the Mind: An Introduction to the Mental Lexicon*, Oxford: Blackwell.

Aizawa, H. (1985) *Ano kuni kono kuni, konna kookoku* (*That Country This Country, Such Advertisements*), Tokyo: Dentsu.

Allwood, J. (1976) *Linguistic Communication as Action and Cooperation: A Study in Pragmatics*, Gothenburg: Gothenburg monographs in linguistics 2, University of Gothenburg Press.

Amano, Y. (1984) 'Kookoku 1984' (Advertisement 1984), in Amano, Y. (ed.) *Kookoku Hihyoo 67* (*Advertising Critiques* 67), Tokyo: Madora Shuppan.

Amano, Y. (1985) *Kookoku no kotoba [kiiwaado]* (*The Language of Advertising [Keywords]*), Tokyo: Dentsu.

Amano, Y. (1986) *Watashi no CM wotchingu* (*My CM Watching*), Tokyo: Asahi Press.

Amano, Y. (1988) *Watashi no CM wotchingu '86–'88* (*MY CM Watching '86–'88*), Tokyo: Asahi Press.

Amano, Y. (1990) *Watashi no CM wotchingu '88–'90* (*My CM Watching '88–'90*), Tokyo: Asahi Press.

Asahi Advertising Prize 1983 (1984) Tokyo: Asahi Press.

Asahi Advertising Prize 1984 (1985) Tokyo: Asahi Press.

Attridge, D. (1988) 'Unpacking the portmanteau, or who's afraid of *Finnegans Wake?*', in Culler, J. (ed.) 140–55.

Augarde, T. (1984) *The Oxford Guide to Word Games*, Oxford: Oxford University Press.

Austin, J. (1962) *How to Do Things with Words*, Oxford: Clarendon Press.

Bach, K. and Harnish R. (1979) *Linguistic Communication And Speech Acts*, Cambridge, Mass.: The MIT Press.

Baehr, H. (ed.) (1980) *Women And Media*, Oxford: Pergamon Press.

Barthes, R. (1984a) *Mythologies*, translated from the French 1954–6 by Lavers, A., London: Granada.

Barthes, R. (1984b) 'Rhetoric of the image', translated from the French 1964 by Heath, S., in Barthes, R. 1984c, 32–51.

Barthes, R. (1984c) *Image Music Text*, translated and selected from the French 1961–71, by Heath, S., London: Fontana.

BIBLIOGRAPHY

Barthes, R. (1985) *Elements of Semiology*, translated from the French 1964 by Lavers, A. and Smith, C., New York: Hill and Wang.

Batsleer, J., Davis, T., O'Rourke, R. and Weedon, C. (1985) *Rewriting English: Cultural Politics of Gender And Class*, London: Methuen.

Beaugrande, R. de and Dressler, W. (1981) *Introduction to Text Linguistics*, London: Longman.

Bencherif, S. (in preparation) 'Linguistics and politics: theories of language interpretation and political discourse', University of London Ph.D. thesis.

Bencherif, S. and Tanaka, K. (1987) 'Covert forms of communication', paper given at the Autumn Meeting of The Linguistic Association of Great Britain, Bradford, September.

Bennett, J. (1976) *Linguistic Behaviour*, Cambridge: Cambridge University Press.

Berger, J. (1984) *Ways of Seeing*, Harmondsworth: Penguin.

Black, M. (1979) 'More about metaphor', in Ortony, A. (ed.), 19–45.

Blakemore, D. (1987) *Semantic Constraints on Relevance*, Oxford: Blackwell.

Blakemore, D. (1992) *Understanding Utterances: An Introduction to Pragmatics*, Oxford: Blackwell.

Blonsky, M. (ed.) (1985) *On Signs: A Semiotic Reader*, Oxford: Blackwell.

Boer, S. and Lycan, W. (1975) 'The myth of semantic presupposition', in Zwicky, A. (ed.) *Working Papers in Linguistics 21*, Columbus, Ohio: Ohio State University Department of Linguistics.

Bolinger, D. (1965) 'The atomization of meaning', *Language 41*, 555–73.

Bolinger, D. (1980) *Language - the Loaded Weapon: The Use And Abuse of Language Today*, London: Longman.

Brown, G. and Yule, G. (1983) *Discourse Analysis*, Cambridge: Cambridge University Press.

Burchill, J. (1986) *Girls of Film*, London: Virgin.

Carnap, R. (1956) *Meaning And Necessity*, London: The University of Chicago Press.

Carston, R. (1988a) 'Language and cognition', in Newmeyer, F. (ed.) vol. 3, 38-68.

Carston, R. (1988b) 'Implicature, explicature and truth-theoretic semantics', in Kempson, R. (ed.), 155–82.

Carston, R. (1994) 'Syntax and pragmatics', in Asher, R.E. (ed.) *The Encyclopaedia of Language And Linguistics vol.8*, Aberdeen: Pergamon Press, 4481–7.

Chiaro, D. (1992) *The Language of Jokes: Analysing Verbal Play*, London: Routledge.

Clark, H. (1982) 'The relevance of common ground: comments on Sperber and Wilson's paper', in Smith, N. (ed.), 124–31.

Clark, H. and Carlson, T. (1981) 'Context for comprehension', in Long, J. and Baddeley, A. (eds) *Attention And Performance IX*, Hillsdale, NJ: L. Erlbaum, 313–30.

Clark, H. and Marshall, C. (1981) 'Definite reference and mutual knowledge', in Joshi, A., Webber, B. and Sag, I. (eds), 10–63.

Clark, H. and Schunk, D. (1980) 'Polite responses to polite requests', *Cognition 8*(2), 111–43.

Cole, P. (ed.) (1978) *Syntax And Semantics 9: Pragmatics,* New York: Academic Press.

Cole, P. (ed.) (1981) *Radical Pragmatics,* New York: Academic Press.

Cole, P. and Morgan, J. (eds) (1975) *Syntax And Semantics 3: Speech Acts,* New York: Academic Press.

Coleman, L. and Kay, P. (1981) 'Prototype semantics: the English word lie', *Language* 57(1), 26–44.

Coltheart, M. (1984) 'Sensory memory: a tutorial review', in Bouma, H. and Bouwhuis, D. (eds) *Attention And Performance X: Control of Language Processes,* London: Lawrence Erlbaum Associates, 257–85.

Condon, J. (1991) *A Half Step Behind: Japanese Women Today,* Tokyo: Charles E. Tuttle.

Cook, G. (1992) *The Discourse of Advertising,* London: Routledge.

Cooper, D. (1986) *Metaphor,* Oxford: Blackwell.

Corke, A. (1986) *Advertising And Public Relations: For Executives Who Want to Acquire Essential New Management Skills to Develop Their Careers,* London: Pan Books.

Coward, R. and Ellis, J. (1977) *Language And Materialism,* London: Routledge & Kegan Paul.

Crain, S. and Steedman, M. (1985) 'On not being led up the garden path: the use of context by the psychological syntax processor', in Dowty, D., Karttunen, L. and Zwicky, A. (eds) *Natural Language Parsing,* Cambridge: Cambridge University Press, 320–58.

Crompton, A. (1987) *The Craft of Copywriting,* London: Hutchinson.

Crystal, D. and Davy, D. (1983) *Investigating English Style,* Harlow: Longman.

Culler, J. (1983a) *The Pursuit of Signs: Semiotics, Literature, Deconstruction,* London: Routledge & Kegan Paul.

Culler, J. (1983b) *Barthes,* London: Fontana.

Culler, J. (ed.) (1988) *On Puns,* Oxford: Blackwell.

Davidson, D. (1979) 'What metaphors mean', in Sacks, S. (ed.), 29–46.

Davis, H. and Walton, P. (eds) (1983) *Language, Image, Media,* Oxford: Blackwell.

Dijk, T. van. (1982) *Text and Context: Explorations in the Semantics And Pragmatics of Discourse,* London: Longman.

Dijk, T. van. (ed.) (1985a) *Handbook of Discourse Analysis, Vol. 3: Discourse And Dialogue,* London: Academic Press.

Dijk, T. van. (ed.) (1985b) *Handbook of Discourse Analysis, Vol. 4: Discourse Analysis in Society,* London: Academic Press.

Douglas, M. (1968) 'The social control of cognition: some factors in joke perception', *Man* 3, 361–76.

Downs, W. (1984) *Language And Society,* London: Fontana.

Dyer, G. (1982) *Advertising as Communication,* London: Methuen.

Eco, U. (1983) *The Role of the Reader,* London: Hutchinson.

Fiske, J. (1984) *Introduction to Communication Studies,* London: Methuen.

Fodor, J. A. (1975) *The Language of Thought,* Cambridge, Mass.: Harvard University Press.

Fodor, J. A. (1981) *Representations*, Cambridge, Mass.: The MIT Press.
Fodor, J. A. (1983) *The Modularity of Mind*, Cambridge, Mass.: The MIT Press.
Fodor, J. A., Garrett, M., Walker, E. and Parkes, C. (1980) 'Against definitions', *Cognition* 8(3), 263–367.
Fodor, J. D. (1977) *Semantics: Theories of Meaning in Generative Grammar*, Brighton: The Harvester Press.
Fodor, J. D., Fodor, J.A. and Garrett, M. (1975)'Psychological unreality of semantic representations', *Linguistic Inquiry* 6, 515–31.
Forceville, C. (1998) *Pictorial Metaphor in Advertising*, London: Routledge.
Fowler, R. (1985) 'Power', in Dijk, T. van (ed.), vol. 4, 61–82.
Fowler, R., Hodge, B., Kress, G. and Trew, T. (1979) *Language And Control*, London: Routledge.
Gazdar, G. (1979) *Pragmatics: Implicature, Presupposition And Logical Form*, New York: Academic Press.
Gazdar, G. and Good, D. (1982) 'On a notion of relevance', in Smith, N. (ed.), 88–100.
Geis, M. (1982) *The Language of Television Advertising*, New York: Academic Press.
Giglioli, P. (ed.) (1972) *Language And Social Context*, Harmondsworth: Penguin.
Goatly, A. (1997) *The Language of Metaphors*, London: Routledge.
Goffman, E. (1976) *Gender Advertisements*, London: Macmillan.
Goffman, E. (1981) *Forms of Talk*, Philadelphia: University of Pennsylvania Press.
Gordon, D. and Lakoff, G. (1975) 'Conversational postulates', in Cole, P. and Morgan, J. (eds), 83–126.
Green, G. and Morgan, J. (1981) 'Pragmatics, grammar and discourse', in Cole, P. (ed.), 167–81.
Greene, J. (1986) *Language Understanding: A Cognitive Approach*, Milton Keynes: Open University Press.
Grice, H. P. (1957) 'Meaning', *Philosophical Review* 66, 377–88.
Grice, H. P. (1968) 'Utterer's meaning and intentions', *Philosophical Review* 78, 147–77.
Grice, H. P. (1975) 'Logic and conversation', in Cole, P. and Morgan, J. (eds), 41–58.
Grice, H. P. (1978) 'Further notes on logic and conversation', in Cole, P. (ed.), 113–28.
Grice, H. P. (1981) 'Presupposition and conversational implicature', in Cole, P. (ed.), 183–98.
Grice, H. P. (1982) 'Meaning revisited', in Smith, N. (ed.), 223–43.
Grice, H. P. (1989) *Studies in the Way of Words*, Cambridge, Mass.: Harvard University Press.
Guiraud, P. (1981) *Semiology*, translated from the French 1971 by Gross, G., London: Routledge & Kegan Paul.
Gumperz, J. (1982) *Discourse Strategies*, Cambridge: Cambridge University Press.
Hakuhodo Institute of Life & Living (ed.) (1987) *Jiryuu wa joryuu (The Trend Is Feminine)*, Tokyo: Nihon Keizai Shinbun Press.

Hall, S., Hobson, D., Lowe, A. and Wills, P. (eds) (1984) *Culture, Media, Language,* London: Hutchinson.

Hawkes, T. (1984) *Metaphor,* London: Methuen.

Hawkes, T. (1985) *Structuralism and Semiotics,* London: Methuen.

Hebdige, D. (1979) *Subculture: The Meaning of Style,* London: Methuen.

Heller, L. (1974) 'Toward a general typology of the pun', *Language And Style* 7, 271-82.

Hickey, Leo (1984) 'Being positive about the negative in advertising', *International Journal of Advertising* 3, 369–72.

Hill, J. (1988) 'Language, culture, and world view', in Newmeyer, F. (ed.), 14–36.

Hoshii, I. (1986) *The World of Sex, vol. 1: Sexual Equality,* Kent: Paul Norobury.

Jakobson, R. (1960) 'Linguistics and poetics', in Sebeok, T. (ed.), 350–77.

Johnson-Laird, P. (1982) 'Mutual ignorance: comments on Clark and Carlson's paper', in Smith, N. (ed.), 40-5.

Jones, J. (1986) *What's in a Name?: Advertising And the Concept of Brands,* Aldershot: Gower.

Joshi, A., Webber, B., and Sag, I. (eds) (1981) *Elements of Discourse Understanding,* Cambridge: Cambridge University Press.

Katz, J. and Fodor, J. (1963) 'The structure of a semantic theory', *Language* 3(2), 170–210.

Kelly, L. (1971) 'Punning and the linguistic sign', *Linguistics* 66, 5–11.

Kempson, R. (1977) *Semantic Theory,* Cambridge: Cambridge University Press.

Kempson, R. (1986) 'Ambiguity and the semantics-pragmatics distinction', in Travis, C. (ed.), 77–103.

Kempson, R. (ed.) (1988) *Mental Representations: The Interface between Language And Reality,* Cambridge: Cambridge University Press.

Kess, J., Copeland, A. and Hoppe, R. (1984) 'Intentional ambiguity as verbal sleight of hand in commercial advertising', *Grazer Linguistische Studien* 22, 147–66.

Key, W. (1973) *Subliminal Seduction,* New York: Signet.

Kinoshita, E. (1988) *Kyacchifureezu no kigoo-ron (Semiotics of Catchphrase),* Osaka: Soogensha.

Kitamura, H., Yamaji, R. and Tabuki, H. (eds) (1981) *Kookoku Kyacchifureezu (Advertising Catchphrase),* Tokyo: Yunhikaku.

Kleinman, P. (1984) (ed.) *World Advertising Review 1985,* London: Cassell.

Kleinman, P. (1990) (ed.) *World Advertising Review 1991,* London: Cassell.

Kress, G. (1985) 'Ideological structures in discourse', in Dijk, T. van (ed.), vol. 4, 27–42.

Kress, G. and Hodge, B. (1979) *Language as Ideology,* London: Routledge & Kegan Paul.

Kumatoridani, T. (1982) 'The structure of persuasive discourse: a cross-cultural analysis of the language in American and Japanese television commercials', Unpublished Ph.D. thesis submitted to Georgetown University.

Labov, W. (1973) 'The boundaries of words and their meanings', in Bailey, C. and Shuy, R. (eds) *New Ways of Analyzing Variation in English*, Washington, DC: Georgetown University Press, 340–71.

Lakoff, G. (1971) 'Hedges: a study in meaning criteria and the logic of fuzzy concepts', *Papers from the 11th Regional Meeting of Chicago Linguistics Society*, Chicago: The University of Chicago Press, 183–228.

Lakoff, G. and Johnson, M. (1980) *Metaphors We Live By*, London: The University of Chicago Press.

Lakoff, R. (1972) 'Language in context', *Language* 48(4), 907–27.

Lakoff, R. (1973) 'Questionable answers and answerable questions', in Kachru, B. *et al.* (eds) *Issues in Linguistics: Papers in Honor of Henry And Renee Kahane*, Urbana: University of Illinois Press, 453–67.

Lakoff, R. (1975) *Language And Woman's Place*, New York: Harper & Row.

Lakoff, R. (1982) 'Persuasive discourse and ordinary conversation, with examples from advertising', in Tannen, D. (ed.) *Analyzing Discourse: Text And Talk*, Washington, DC: Georgetown University Press, 25–42.

Leach, E. (1964) 'Anthropological aspects of language: animal categories and verbal abuse', in Lenneberg, E. (ed.), *New Directions in the Study of Language*, Cambridge: Cambridge University Press.

Leach, E. (1976) *Culture and Communication: The Logic by Which Symbols are Connected*, Cambridge: Cambridge University Press.

Leech, G. (1996) *English in Advertising: A Linguistic Study of Advertising in Great Britain*, London: Longman.

Leech, G. (1969) *A Linguistic Guide to English Poetry*, London: Longman.

Leech, G. (1981) *Semantics*, 2nd edition, Harmondsworth: Penguin.

Leech, G. (1983) *Principles of Pragmatics*, London: Longman.

Leech, G. and Short, M. (eds) (1984) *Style in Fiction: A Linguistic Introduction to English Fictional Prose*, London: Longman.

Levinson, S. (1979) 'Activity types and language', *Linguistics* 17, 365–99.

Levinson, S. (1983) *Pragmatics*, Cambridge: Cambridge University Press.

Lyons, J. (1977) *Semantics, vols 1 & 2*, Cambridge: Cambridge University Press.

Lyons, J. (1979) *Introduction to Theoretical Linguistics*, Cambridge: Cambridge University Press.

Lyons, J. (1981) *Language, Meaning and Context*, London: Fontana.

McCawley, J. (1978) 'Conversational implicature and the lexicon', in Cole, P. (ed.), 245–59.

Margalit, A. (ed.) (1976) *Meaning And Use*, London: D. Reidel.

Marslen-Wilson, W. and Tyler, L. (1980) 'The temporal structure of spoken language understanding', *Cognition* 8(1), 1–72.

Marslen-Wilson, W. and Tyler, L. (1981) 'Central processes in speech understanding', *Philosophical Transactions of the Royal Society London*, 317–32.

Millum, T. (1975) *Images of Woman: Advertising in Woman's Magazines*, London: Chatto & Windus.

Moeran, B. (1983) 'The language of Japanese tourism', *Annals of Tourism Research* 10, 93-108.

Moeran, B. (1984) 'Individual, group and seishin: Japan's internal cultural debate', *Man* 19, 252–66.

Myers, G. (1994) *Words in Ads*, London: Edward Arnold.

Myers, K. (1983) 'Understanding advertisers', in Davis, H. and Walton, P. (eds), 205-23.

Nash, W. (1985) *The Language of Humour: Style And Technique in Comic Discourse*, London: Longman.

Newmeyer, F. (1985) (ed.) *Linguistics: The Cambridge Survey IV: Language The Socio-cultural Contest*, Cambridge: Cambridge University Press.

Norrick, N. (1984) 'Stock conversational witticisms', *Journal of Pragmatics* 8, 195–209.

Ogden, C. and Richards, I. (1985) *The Meaning of Meaning: A Study of the Influence of Language Upon Thought And the Science of Symbolism*, London: Routledge & Kegan Paul.

Ortony, A. (1979) (ed.) *Metaphor and Thought*, Cambridge: Cambridge University Press.

Packard, V. (1961) *The Status Seekers: An Exploration of Class Behavior in America*, Harmondsworth: Penguin.

Packard, V. (1981) (Edition for the 1980s) *The Hidden Persuaders*, Harmondsworth: Penguin.

Parret, Herman (1983) *Semiotics And Pragmatics*, Amsterdam: John Benjamins.

Pateman, T. (1980) *Language, Truth And Politics: Towards a Radical Theory of Communication*, London: John Stroud.

Pateman, T. (1981) 'Communicating with computer programs', *Language and Communication* 1, 3–12.

Pateman, T. (1983) 'How is understanding an advertisement possible?', in Davis, H. and Walton, P. (eds), 187–204.

Pateman, T. (1987) *Language in Mind And Language in Society*, Oxford: Clarendon Press.

Pearson, J. and Turner, G. (1966) *The Persuasion Industry*, Readers Union: Eyre & Spottiswoode.

Pulman, S. (1983) *Word Meaning And Belief*, London: Croom Helm.

Raskin, V. (1985) *Semantic Mechanisms of Humor*, Dordrecht: D. Reidel.

Redfern, W. (1982)'Guano of the mind: puns in advertising', *Language and Communication* 2(3), 269–76.

Redfern, W. (1984) *Puns*, Oxford: Blackwell.

Rey, G. (1983) 'Concepts and stereotypes', *Cognition* 15, 237–62.

Ricoeur, P. (1986) *The Rule of Metaphor: Multi-Disciplinary Studies of the Creation of Meaning in Language*, translated by Czerny, R., London: Routledge & Kegan Paul.

Roth, I. and Frisby, J. (1986) *Perception And Representation: A Cognitive Approach*, Milton Keynes: Open University Press.

Rumelhart, D. (1979) 'Some problems with the notion of literal meaning', in Ortony, A. (ed.), 78–91.

Rusiecki, J. (1985) *Adjectives And Comparison in English: A Semantic Study*, London: Longman.

Sacks, H. (1974) 'An analysis of the course of a joke's telling in conversation', in Bawman, R. and Sherzer, J. (eds), *Exploration in the Ethnography of Speaking*, Cambridge: Cambridge University Press, 337–53.

Sacks, S. (ed.) (1979) *On Metaphor*, Chicago: The University of Chicago Press.

Sadock, J. (1978) 'On testing for conversational implicature', in Cole, P. (ed.), 281–97.

Saussure, F. de (1974) *Course in General Linguistics*, translated from the French 1916 by Baskin, W., Oxford: Peter Owen.

Schank, R. and Abelson, R. (1977) 'Script, plans and knowledge', in Johnson-Laird P. and Wason, P. (eds) *Thinking: Readings in Cognitive Science*, Cambridge: Cambridge University Press, 412–32.

Schiffer, S. (1972) *Meaning*, Oxford: Clarendon Press.

Schmidt, R. and Kess, J. (1986) *Television Advertising And Televangelism: Discourse Analysis of Persuasive Language*, Amsterdam: John Benjamins.

Schon, D. (1979) 'Generative metaphor: a perspective on problem-setting in social policy', in Ortony, A. (ed.), 254–83.

Schudson, M. (1984) *Advertising, the Uneasy Persuasion: Its Dubious Impact on American Society*, New York: Basic Books.

Searle, J. (ed.) (1971) *The Philosophy of Language*, Oxford: Oxford University Press.

Searle, J. (1976) 'Intentionality and the use of language', in Margalit, A. (ed.), 181–97.

Searle, J. (1979) 'Metaphor', in Ortony, A. (ed.), 92–123.

Searle, J. (1983) *Intentionality*, Cambridge: Cambridge University Press.

Sebeok, T. (ed.) (1960) *Style in Language*, Cambridge, Mass.: The MIT Press.

Seidal, G. (1985) 'Political discourse analysis', in Dijk, T. van (ed.), vol. 4, 43–59.

Sherry, J. (1987) 'May your life be marvellous: English language labelling and the semiotics of Japanese promotion', *Journal of Consumer Research* 14, 178–88.

Shezer, J. (1978) 'Oh! That's a pun and I didn't mean it', *Semiotica* 22(3/4), 335–50.

Shezer, J. (1985) 'Puns and jokes', in Dijk, T. van (ed.), vol. 3, 213–21.

Shimamori, M. (1984) *Kookoku no naka no onna-tachi (Women in Advertising)*, Tokyo: Yamato Shoboo.

Sinclair, J. and Coulthard, R. (1975) *Towards an Analysis of Discourse: The English Used by Teachers And Pupils*, Oxford: Oxford University Press.

Smith, N. (ed.) (1982) *Mutual Knowledge*, London: Academic Press.

Smith, N. and Wilson, D. (1992) 'Introduction', *Lingua* 87, 1–10.

Smith, R. (1987) 'Gender inequality in contemporary Japan', *Journal of Japanese Studies* 13(1), 1–25.

Spender, D. (1985) *Man Made Language*, 2nd edition, London: Routledge & Kegan Paul.

Sperber, D. (1984) *Rethinking Symbolism*, Cambridge: Cambridge University Press.

Sperber, D. (1988) 'Word meaning and concept', paper given at a workshop on Relevance Theory, University of Essex, June.

Sperber, D. and Wilson, D. (1981a) 'Irony and the use-mention distinction', in Cole, P. (ed.), 295–318.

Sperber D. and Wilson, D. (1981b) 'Pragmatics', *Cognition* 10(4), 281–6.
Sperber D. and Wilson, D. (1982) 'Mutual knowledge and relevance in theories of comprehension', in Smith, N. (ed.), 61–131.
Sperber, D. and Wilson, D. (1986a) *Relevance: Communication And Cognition*, Oxford: Blackwell.
Sperber, D. and Wilson, D. (1986b) 'Loose talk', *Proceedings of the Aristotelian Society* NS LXXXVI, 153–71.
Sperber, D. and Wilson, D. (1987a) 'Precis of relevance, and presumptions of relevance', *Behavioral and Brain Sciences* 10(4), 697–10.
Sperber, D. and Wilson, D. (1987b) 'Authors' response', *Behavioral and Brain Sciences* 10(4), 736–54.
Sperber, D. and Wilson, D. (1990) 'Linguistic form and relevance', *UCL Working Papers in Linguistics* 2, 95–112.
Sperber, D. and Wilson, D. (1995) *Relevance: Communication And Cognition*, 2nd edition, Oxford: Blackwell.
Strawson, P. (1971) 'Intention and convention in speech acts', in Searle, J. (ed.), 23–38.
Suzuki, Y. (1975) 'Onna to ryuukoo' (Women and fashion), in Nihon-jin Kenkyuukai (ed.) *Nihon-jin Kenkyuu 3: Onna ga kangaete-iru-koto (A study of the Japanese 3: What women are thinking about)*, Tokyo: Shiseido.
Tanaka, K. (1990a) ' "Intelligent elegance": women in Japanese advertising', in Ben-Ari, E., Moeran, B. and Balentine, J. (eds) *Unwrapping Japan*, Manchester: Manchester University Press, 78–96.
Tanaka, K. (1990b) 'Accounting for differences in covert communication: a Relevance approach', paper given at the Autumn Meeting of The Linguistic Association of Great Britain, Leeds, September.
Tanaka, K. (1992) 'The pun in advertising: a pragmatic approach', *Lingua* 87, 91–102.
Tanaka, K. (1993a) 'The language of perfume advertising', paper given at the Japan Research Centre seminar, School of Oriental and African Studies on 3 March 1993.
Tanaka, K. (1993b) 'The notion of "wildness" in Japanese advertising', paper given at the 7th Meeting of Japan Anthropology Workshop, Baniff, Canada, April 1993.
Tanaka, K. (1995) '*Kookoku o yomitoku*' (Deciphering advertisements), *Gengo (Language)* 24(4), 48–55.
Tanaka, K. (1998) 'Japanese women's magazines: the language of aspirations', in Martinez, D. (ed.) *The World of Japanese Popular Culture: Gender, Shifting Boundaries And Global Cultures*, Cambridge/ Melbourne: Cambridge University Press, 110–32.
Tarlo, E. (1986) 'Semiotics of perfume', unpublished undergraduate dissertation submitted to School of Oriental and African Studies, University of London.
Travis, C. (ed.) (1986) *Meaning And Interpretation*, Oxford: Blackwell.
Vestergaard, T. and Schrøder, K. (1985) *The Language of Advertising*, Oxford: Blackwell.
West, C. and Zimmerman, D. (1985) 'Gender, language, and discourse', in Dijk, T. van (ed.), vol.4, 103–24.
Widdowson, P. (1982) (ed.) *Re-reading English,* London: Methuen.

BIBLIOGRAPHY

Williams, Raymond (1981) *Keywords: A Vocabulary of Culture And Society*, London: Fontana.

Williamson, Judith (1983) *Decoding Advertisements: Ideology And Meaning in Advertising*, London: Marion Boyars.

Wilson, D. and Sperber, D. (1981) 'On Grice's theory of conversation', in Werth, P. (ed.) *Conversation And Discourse*, London: Croom Helm, 155–78.

Wilson, D. and Sperber, D. (1986) 'Inference and implicature', in Travis, C. (ed.), 45–75.

Wilson, D. and Sperber, D. (1988a) 'Mood and the analysis of nondeclarative sentences', in Dancy, J., Moravcsik, J. and Taylor, C. (eds) *Language And Value*, Stanford, Calif.: Stanford University Press, 229–324.

Wilson, D. and Sperber, D. (1988b) 'Representation and relevance', in Kempson, R. (ed.), 133–53.

Wilson, J. (1990) *Politically Speaking*, Oxford: Blackwell.

Wright, R. (1975) 'Meaning-nn and conversational implicature', in Cole, P. and Morgan, J. (eds), 363–82.

Yamakawa, K. and Nakamura, A. (1985) *Waadhingu 100 soo (Wording 100 Ideas)*, Tokyo: Dentsu.

Yamamoto, A. and Amano, Y. (1983) *Kookoku o manabu hito no tameni (For People Who Study Advertising)*, Tokyo: Sekaishisoosha.

Yoshida, S. (1990) 'A government-based analysis of the "more" in Japanese', *Phonology* 7(2), 331–51.

INDEX

accessibility 4, 17, 26, 30–2, 62, 66–7, 72–4, 81, 122, 125, 130
'activity type' 7–9
Aftate advertisement 11
All Nippon Airways advertisement 73–4, 76–8
Amariage advertisement 102–3
ambiguity 15, 60–2, 97, 132
'anchorage' 2–3
Anholt, S. 62
Armstrong, R. 38–9
Asahi Advertising Prize 126, 128
assumption(s) 7, 17–19, 22–3, 26–31, 34, 37–8, 41–2, 45–6, 55, 58, 79, 90, 92, 96–8, 110, 126; contextual 26–7, 75, 123; implicated 73, 81–2; strengthening of existing 23; elimination of old 23
attention 3, 22–3, 42, 51, 58, 64–5, 68–9, 71, 76, 80, 82, 94, 105–6; request for 19–20, 24–5
Attridge, D. 60–1

Bach, K. 17
'baldness paradox' 109
Barthes, R. 1–4
Bencherif, S. xiii, 41, 88–9
Benetton advertisement 4
Blakemore, D. 7, 27, 86
Boer, S. 9
Bosch Telecom advertisement 74
Brown, G. 17

Budget advertisement 74

calculability 10, 21–2, 86–7
Can Cam 107, 113
Carnap, R. 108
Carston, R. xiii, 7, 27
Cellnet advertisement 74–5
central thought processes 2
Christian Lacroix advertisement 56
chunk 104
Citizen advertisement 122–3
classificatory concept *see* concept
co-operation: cognitive 37; social 36–40, 42–3, 59
co-operative principle 20–1
Coca-Cola advertisement 74
code 1–3, 16, 26
cognition 22, 41
cognitive environment 18, 41–3, 58, 106
Collin's English Dictionary 83
communication: covert (non-ostensive) xii, 19, 26, 29, 34, 40–6, 54–6, 58, 75–6, 132; explicit 4, 26, 73; implicit 26, 32; linguistic 4; non-linguistic 4, 55; overt (ostensive) 19–20, 29, 37–42, 51, 75–7, 132; and social implications 36–7, 42–5, 58, 71; subliminal 44, 51; theory of 12, 14; weak 38–9, 42, 89, 94, 132; *see also* inferential